Praise for *40 Days of Farming*

"As a renowned leader and innovator in real estate, John McMonigle continuously strives to reinvent and reimagine the industry. With *40 Days of Farming*, he gives readers the everyday tools they need to launch a successful career based upon his proven system of geographic farming, as well as the 'countercultural' values of love, faith, and hope."

—Tony Robbins, #1 *New York Times* bestselling author of *Unshakable: Your Guide to Financial Freedom* and *Money: Master the Game*

"John McMonigle has proven time and time again that he possesses the elite knowledge and wisdom necessary to be profoundly successful in the real estate industry. His dedication to pushing the envelope when it comes to proprietary technology and marketing strategies has enabled him to become one of the most influential and successful real estate experts in the world today. With *40 Days of Farming*, John has created a simple, yet disciplined path to attaining both real estate and personal success for new and experienced real estate agents around the globe."

—Tom Ferry, #1 ranked Real Estate Educator by Swanepoel Power 200 and bestselling author of *Life! By Design* and *Mindset, Model and Marketing!*

"In *40 Days of Farming*, John McMonigle unveils the secret to his success through the art of geographic farming and dedication to his faith. This workbook lays out exactly what needs to be done to realize financial and spiritual success as a real estate agent, and empowers readers to take control of their future. *40 Days of Farming* provides agents with a business and life plan, allowing them to progress and lay the foundation for success in 40 days."

—David Cabot, Former President and CEO of Berkshire Hathaway HomeServices California Properties

40 DAYS OF FARMING

UNLOCK THE SECRET TO REAL ESTATE SUCCESS AND PERSONAL FULFILLMENT

JOHN McMONIGLE

Matt Holt Books
An Imprint of BenBella Books, Inc.
Dallas, TX

BenBella Books, Inc.
10440 N. Central Expressway
Suite 800
Dallas, TX 75231
benbellabooks.com
Send feedback to feedback@benbellabooks.com

BenBella and *Matt Holt* are federally registered trademarks.

Printed in the United States of America
10 9 8 7 6 5 4 3 2 1

Library of Congress Control Number: 2021040489
ISBN 9781637741054
eISBN 9781637741061

Copyediting by Jennifer Brett Greenstein
Proofreading by Sarah Vostok and Jenny Bridges
Text design and composition by PerfecType, Nashville, TN
Cover design by Brigid Pearson
Cover photo by Adam Dubich Photography
Author photo by Amy Whitcomb
Printed by Lake Book Manufacturing

Special discounts for bulk sales are available.
Please contact bulkorders@benbellabooks.com.

To my earthly father, who loved and supported me like none other.

*To my mother, who has been a strong spiritual
influence in my life to this day.*

To my brother in Christ, Scott MacDonald, cofounder of Agentinc.

*To my first boss, Tom Woolever, who taught me how to laugh
so hard my sides would split in the 130-degree heat of an
Oklahoma hayfield, and that cold water tastes good even with
a little dirt and bugs mixed in when you're thirsty enough.*

CONTENTS

Days 29–40

 1) Spiritual Health
2) Physical Health

Ground Your "Smart Goals" in Love

 3) Mental Health
4) Emotional Health
5) Relational Health

Have Hope in the 7000 Promises in Scripture

 6) Financial Health
7) Vocational Health

Apply Faith to Your "Smart Goals"

RECOMMENDED READING

1) Purpose Driven Life
2) The TB 12 Method
3) Wide Angle – Framing Your Worldview

4) Christians in the Workplace
5) Blueprint for Success

6) Managing Our Finances God's Way
7) Financial Fitness

PREFACE

L ove. Faith. Hope. These three words are the basis of the journey you are about to embark upon. *40 Days of Farming* is a "countercultural" program designed to give you the spiritual, physical, mental, emotional, relational, financial, and vocational health necessary to succeed in today's real estate industry.

But before we get started, it's important to understand that change doesn't come all at once. Many of us realize that there is always room for improvement in our lives both professionally and spiritually. As a result, we look for a painless cure that can get the job done easily. Many of you have probably read a few self-help books and tried to change or enhance your life, only to find yourself reverting back to the way you were before in just a few short months. That's because most self-help books are designed to tell you what to do—but they don't give you the power to accomplish what you are setting out to do. So where do you get the power to achieve your goals? The answer is simple—God. God gives you the power to transform your life and become the successful person He wants you to be.

As Christians, we live in a world that is broken. We live in a world where insurrections, wars, disease, politics, racism, and polarization exist in every country, in every town—and in every industry. But with our "countercultural" Christian beliefs of peace, love, acceptance, and goodwill, we can be instruments used by God to transform the world, ourselves, and our careers in a tremendously positive and influential way. Galatians 5:22–23 says it best: "But the fruit of the Spirit is love, joy, peace, forbearance, kindness, goodness, faithfulness, gentleness and self-control. Against such things there is no law" (NIV).

Corrie ten Boom, a venerated member of the Dutch resistance, once said, "If you look at the world, you'll be distressed. If you look within, you'll be depressed. If you look at God you'll be at rest." *40 Days of Farming* applies Scripture to your career and includes a life plan handed down by God, along with a proven business plan culled from my decades of experience and success in the real estate industry.

It has been said that it takes 40 days to transform your world and create a better one. The proof? Look to Scripture. David conquers Goliath after 40 days of unending war against all odds. Noah builds a new world after 40 straight days and nights of rain and flood. It took Moses 40 days to receive the Ten Commandments, transforming the entire moral fabric of society. Jesus Christ spent 40 days in the Judean Desert, battling temptation, rejecting evil, and ultimately saving the world from a tumultuous future.

Over my years as a real estate agent, I've been able to hone specific talents and methods that have helped me achieve success. *40 Days of Farming* teaches the intricate techniques and processes associated with geographic farming—a proven system of generating productivity based on love and community stewardship. As a real estate agent, you are in the business of transforming lives and guiding others through one of the biggest decisions and transactions of their lives. Your choice to pursue a career in real estate is by definition a selfless act, and your commitment to your craft and becoming successful at it can only help the lives of those you devote your service and time to.

As agents, we must approach our industry and clients with love. We must find our hope in the over 7,000 promises God has made to us in Scripture. We must have faith in all things unseen and in God alone.

It is vitally important to your journey to understand and accept that God is actively looking for people to bless. All we have to do is believe, obey, and put God first—it is a mission to do the work of Christ. And if we adhere to our Christian faith and bind Scripture to our hearts, we will be rewarded not only here on earth but also in the Kingdom of Heaven. But how do we become successful both spiritually and professionally? What's the one thing that can transform our lives? The answer: His Word, First Word. His Word, Last Word. God has provided us with a precise pathway to success, fulfillment, and happiness. By looking to Scripture at the start and end of each and every day, we can gain the knowledge and spiritual capacity needed to succeed, just as God intended us to.

Joshua 1:8 is a promise from God. It reads, "Keep this Book of the Law always on your lips; meditate on it day and night, so that you may be careful to do everything written in it. Then you will be prosperous and successful" (NIV). By grasping hold of and having faith in the 7,000 promises made to you in Scripture, you are allowing yourself to be blessed by God with the success you desire and the spiritual peace you seek. By committing yourself to *40 Days of Farming*, you are actively allowing God to help you manage and expand your business, all while providing an immensely important service to clients that can transform their lives in one of the most positive ways imaginable.

10 Laws of Planting

1. Everything Starts with a Seed

Think of this book as a seed. From *40 Days of Farming*, you will grow into a more successful and spiritual agent.

> "Then God said, 'Let the land produce vegetation: seed-bearing plants and trees on the land that bear fruit with seed in it, according to their various kinds.' And it was so."
>
> **Genesis 1:11 (NIV)**

2. A Seed Has No Power Until It Is Planted

The power of this book can be realized only by your dedication to rooting yourself in the techniques and spiritual guidelines found within.

> "Very truly I tell you, unless a kernel of wheat falls to the ground and dies, it remains only a single seed. But if it dies, it produces many seeds. Anyone who loves their life will lose it, while anyone who hates their life in this world will keep it for eternal life."
>
> **John 12:24–25 (NIV)**

"Does a farmer always plow and never plant? Is he forever cultivating his soil but never planting it? No! . . . The farmer knows just what to do, for God has given him understanding."

Isaiah 28:24, 26 (NLT)

3. Some Seed Should Be Planted Instead of Eaten

40 Days of Farming is designed to help you grow as a real estate agent and as a servant of God. Take this knowledge and use it to expand your business and spiritual self.

"Because the famine was so severe, everyone in Egypt sold their land to Pharaoh. Then Joseph told them this: 'I will provide you with seed so you can plant crops. Then, when you harvest it, you are to give 20 percent of it back to the King, and you get to keep 80 percent. But don't eat all your seed! Use your seed to plant next year's crops, so you can feed your family in the future.' The people replied, 'You've saved our lives!'"

Genesis 47:20–25

"Now he who supplies seed to the sower and bread for food will also supply and increase your store of seed and will enlarge the harvest of your righteousness.

2 Corinthians 9:10 (NIV)

4. Whatever I Plant Is What I Harvest

By grounding your career and self in love, faith, and hope, you will harvest love, faith, and hope. Remain positive about your journey, and you will see a positive change in all facets of your life.

"Now he who supplies seed to the sower and bread for food will also supply and increase your store of seed and will enlarge the harvest of your righteousness."

2 Corinthians 9:10 (NIV)

"A wicked person earns deceptive wages, but the one who sows righteousness reaps a sure reward."

Proverbs 22:8 (NLT)

"If you plant the good seeds of righteousness, you'll harvest a crop of my love. So plow up the hard ground of your hearts, for now is the time to seek the Lord, so that he may come and shower goodness on you like rain."

Hosea 10:12 (NLT)

5. I'm Not the Only One Planting Seeds in My Life.

You are surrounded by other agents, friends, loved ones, children, ancestors, and others who have influenced you in both positive and negative ways. Understand that your decisions affect those around you, just as their decisions affect you. By becoming a better agent and better person, you are planting seeds of growth and opportunity not only for yourself but also for those surrounding you.

"I sent you to reap what you have not worked for. Others have done the hard work, and you have reaped the benefits of their labor."

John 4:38 (NIV)

6. I Harvest in a Different Season Than I Plant In

Today, you have planted your seed. By day 40, you will have experienced a transformation. But remember, you may not feel this transformation happening each day. Be patient and trust in the over 7,000 promises God has made in Scripture dedicated to your success and happiness.

"There is a time for everything, and a season for every activity under heavens . . . A time to plant and a time to uproot . . . A time to scatter stones and a time to gather them . . ."

Ecclesiastes 3:1–5 (NIV)

7. I Always Harvest More Than I Plant

One orange tree seed will provide countless oranges over its life-time. *40 Days of Farming* can provide valuable opportunities, spir-itual guidance, and information over your lifetime.

> "Isaac planted crops in that land and the same year reaped a hundredfold, because the Lord blessed him."
>
> **Genesis 26:12 (NIV)**

> "I sent you to reap what you have not worked for. Others have done the hard work, and you have reaped the benefits of their labor."
>
> **Mark 4:8 (NIV)**

8. I Increase My Harvest by Planting More Seed

40 Days of Farming teaches you to be generous and to use your wealth and success for the greater good. By embodying love, faith, and hope in your everyday life, you will generate greater love, faith, and hope in yourself.

> "Remember this: Whoever sows sparingly will also reap spar-ingly, and whoever sows generously will also reap generously. Each of you should give what you have decided in your heart to give, not reluctantly or under compulsion, for God loves a cheerful giver."
>
> **2 Corinthians 9:6–7 (NIV)**

> "The world of the generous gets larger and larger; the world of the stingy gets smaller and smaller."
>
> **Proverbs 11:24 (MSG)**

9. I Should Always Be Planting Good Seeds

40 Days of Farming is built to give you the strength and health you need to develop into a better agent and better person.

"Those who wait for perfect conditions will never plant seeds; and those who look at every cloud will never reap a harvest."

Ecclesiastes 11:4 (NCV)

"Do your planting in the morning and in the evening, too! You never know whether it will all grow well or whether one planting will do better than the other."

Ecclesiastes 11:6 (TEV)

10. While Waiting for My Harvest, I Must Be Patient and Not Give Up

Dedicate yourself to the knowledge within this book and trust in its transformative effect not only throughout these next 40 days but also throughout your lifetime.

"Let us not become weary in doing good, for at the proper time we will reap a harvest if we do not give up."

Galatians 6:9 (NIV)

"Those who plant in tears will harvest with shouts of joy. They weep as they go to plant their seed, but they sing as they return with the harvest!"

Psalm 126:5–6 (NLT)

"Your hearts have become hard, like an unplowed field where weeds have taken over. So plow up the hard ground of your hearts! Do not waste good seed by planting among weeds."

Jeremiah 4:3 (CEV & NLT)

7 PRINCIPLES OF HEALTH

A gentinc. was built by agents, for agents. We are dedicated to providing you with the resources you need to succeed not only in real estate but also in your personal life. Through Scripture, God has given you the blueprint to live and maintain a healthy, successful, and happy existence grounded in the three "countercultural" pillars of love, faith, and hope. In order to become the best version of yourself, it is important to recognize and maintain these seven principles of personal and communal health:

- Spiritual
- Physical
- Mental
- Emotional
- Relational
- Financial
- Vocational

By devoting yourself to improving your health both physically and spiritually, you are laying down a clear path to reaching your maximum potential. Remember, whatever dreams you have, God has bigger ones for you.

Spiritual Health

God created you in His image. You have the capacity to better yourself and those around you by placing your faith in God and putting Him first in all your personal, financial, spiritual, and professional decisions. It's important to remember that God is your business partner. It is vital to your success to consult with Him and trust Him in each endeavor you embark upon.

Physical Health

Understand that God is loaning your body to you while you dwell here on earth. Because of this, He expects you to take good care of yourself, to eat healthy, to take part in wholesome activities, to be proud of your body, and to encourage your friends and loved ones to be active and live a sound lifestyle. Remember, your health affects everyone around you—your family, your loved ones, and your colleagues are all depending on you to be present, capable, and productive each and every day.

Mental Health

Love. Faith. Hope. Each of these "countercultural" values was created by God to ensure that you live a fulfilled and fruitful life. By understanding your purpose, placing God first, believing in the over 7,000 promises of Scripture, and continuously striving for personal growth through new experiences, insight, and knowledge, you are working toward creating a harmonious relationship with God.

Emotional Health

Maintaining emotional health allows you to remain connected to your social environment and provide guidance for your family and loved ones. By accepting those of different faiths and different opinions, as well as learning from your mistakes and looking to God for guidance, you can positively contribute to your community and lead by example.

Relational Health

God created you to be socially active and to help others. Your relational health is important to maintain friendships and faith, as well as to serve your community and church. By actively participating in the Christian community, you can better serve the world and those in need, as well as expand your understanding of the human condition and improve your personal and professional relationships.

Financial Health

There are more verses in the Bible on money and finances than on any other subject. Why? Because God has big dreams for you, and He wants you to succeed. He wants you to enjoy your life here on earth responsibly and to use your financial health to spread the message of love, faith, and hope across the world. He wants you to be in a position to help those in need. By asking God to be your business partner, by giving Him access to all your financial decisions, and by tithing and saving, you are investing not only in your financial success here on earth but also in the Kingdom of Heaven.

Vocational Health

As an agent, you are inherently a steward of your community. You are actively assisting many of your clients through the biggest financial decision of their lives and creating better, brighter futures for them. By dedicating your life to expanding your abilities, as well as utilizing your talents, knowledge, and expertise to benefit your clients, you are creating an environment founded upon love, faith, and hope. You have been blessed as an agent. Take the gifts God has given you, and use them to create a better world for yourself, your family, and your community.

Love is patient and kind; love does not envy or boast; it is not arrogant or rude. It does not insist on its own way; it is not irritable or resentful; it does not rejoice at wrongdoing, but rejoices with the truth. Love bears all things, believes all things, hopes all things, endures all things. (ESV)

1 Corinthians 13:4–7

Days
1-14

PAINT YOUR VISION

The plans of the diligent lead to profit as surely as haste leads to poverty. (NIV)

Proverbs 21:5

Whenever I speak to agents and executives, I ask them what their vision of success is. Nine times out of ten, they can't answer the question. They may say "money," "legacy," "retirement," or "a boat"—but that isn't the full picture, is it? The truth is, we think we know what success is, but in actuality we have never defined it and we have never embedded this definition and vision within ourselves.

Renowned former UCLA basketball coach John Wooden said, "Success is peace of mind that is the direct result of self-satisfaction in knowing you did your best to become the best that you are capable of becoming."

A humanistic identity of success is generally a combination of three ingredients:

- Money
- Fame
- Power

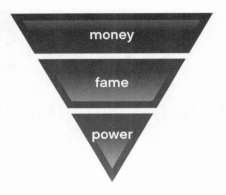

These words sound nice—who doesn't want money, fame, and power? But it's important to remember that you can earn or inherit millions of dollars and your life can still be an absolute disappointment. You can become world famous and still fail miserably at life. You can have great power and far-reaching influence only to become a narcissistic dolt. Celebrities, world leaders, corporate magnates, and tech billionaires show us these unfavorable possible outcomes each and every day—just watch TMZ! So what's the solution? Putting God first in your life. A Christian identity of success is made of three different ingredients:

- Loving and knowing God
- Binding Scripture to our hearts
- Finding and fulfilling God's divine will for our lives

True success is caring about and holding the attention of an audience of one—God—and doing our best to become what He has created us to be. What we can recognize in Scripture and in the Old Testament is that the great followers of God dating back to the days of Abraham, Isaac, Jacob, Job, David, and Solomon were blessed with both a humanistic and Christian identity of success. Their lives and their paths combined elements of both identities, allowing them to change the world for the better while remaining devoted to the will of God. In short, God blessed them in every way.

You are about to embark on a journey that can potentially change the rest of your life for the better, bringing a sense of fulfillment, service, and comfort to you and your family. You have taken the first step toward achieving success both in your career and your personal life. But in order to achieve these goals, it is important to commit yourself wholly to your vision, to create a plan, to practice patience, and to find the discipline and determination to bring your ideals to fruition. In short, you must become the best that you are capable of being.

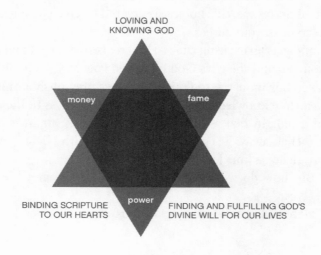

So how do you define success, understand it, and achieve it? How do you become the best that you are capable of becoming?

Let's start with the concept of visualization. Visualization is defined as simply the formation of a mental image. Sure, we can all form a mental image whenever we want to—that isn't too difficult to accomplish. But to truly see your future and to believe in this mental image of your future is an integral component of succeeding in your real estate and spiritual endeavors.

For example, if you were to set out on a journey through an unfamiliar forest, you'd most likely bring a detailed map along with you. This map would provide you with direction, physical markers, and information on where to find water and shelter. But this map would also provide you with much more—it would provide comfort and it would help you believe you were on the right path, that you were heading toward a tangible destination and that in the end you would find your way.

Our lives and careers are no different. Striking out on a new path requires a spiritual and physical blueprint to help you along the way. Our world is filled with these blueprints, and much has been written about finding purpose, following the path, and envisioning a tangible future. Just as God has given you a map in the form of Scripture, this book was created to give you a map of what is to come in your career.

Today is an exciting time to be a real estate agent and to believe in yourself and the gifts God has given you. New technologies have allowed our industry to flourish in ways previously unimaginable. A wealth of knowledge is at our fingertips. Access to the most brilliant minds in real estate, physics, astronomy, finance, and art is just a click away. The ability to network with clients and market your talents is limitless.

But how do we visualize what we want from our career and ourselves?

Here's an exercise to get you started:

Pinterest Exercise

Vision boards can be an effective tool when it comes to visualizing future success. In fact, the vision board can be used as a life metaphor—meaning we can use these visual aids to symbolize and represent our ideal environments. Pinterest is an easy platform that allows you to select visual references that can assist you in imagining your life 1, 2, 5, 10, or 20 years from now. In order to realize these goals and manifestations, it's important to see and feel a tangible representation of them. If you can feel it, touch it, taste it, smell it, and see it, then it must be real, right?

First, create a Pinterest account and begin pinning physical and spiritual representations of your future to your board. Think about what kind of a person you want to be. Think about what is vital to you. Think about what you need to live a full and happy life, and determine which things are luxuries and which things are necessities. Think about the color palette of your life, the things you want to touch, the emotions you want to feel when your eyes open in the morning.

As you continue to add images to your vision board, be sure to take a step back every now and again and look at the world you've created. Are all the things you see in front of you what you truly want out of your life? Are they functional? Do they bring happiness not only to you but to the ones you love?

When you feel satisfied with your vision of the future, put it aside for a moment, or a day, or a week. Then, when you are ready, reevaluate your goals with God and your spirit in mind, and make the adjustments you feel are necessary to visualize a whole existence, personally, financially, and spiritually.

Now, if after your Pinterest exercise you feel conflicted about striving for financial and personal gain as a follower of Christ, understand that being a successful agent or broker is a true act of servitude. Many people will depend on you to help them make some of the biggest decisions of their lives—to guide them toward a better future for themselves, their spouses, their children, and someday, their grandchildren. To be a present and integral piece of the future for so many people is inherently a selfless act, an act that brings about a positive change across a wide spectrum, including your own self and family.

> Command those who are rich in this present world not to be arrogant nor to put their hope in wealth, which is so uncertain, but to put their hope in God, who richly provides us with everything for our enjoyment. Command them to do good, to be rich in good deeds, and to be generous and willing to share. In this way they will lay up treasure for themselves as a firm foundation for the coming age, so that they may take hold of the life that is truly life. (NIV)
>
> **1 Timothy 6:17–19**

Remember, no matter how big your dreams are, God's dreams for you are bigger. So go ahead and pin that dream to your board—if you walk in the path of God and devote yourself to a life of servitude, you are creating a bright and positive light in the world that has a far-reaching affect. And during this process, it's okay to change and redefine your idea of success—as long as you have a clear picture of where you want to go.

Today is the beginning of a brighter future with Agentinc. Be proud that you have decided to achieve greatness in your field, to take the first step toward realizing your personal and financial goals, and to provide a vital service for those who depend on you.

> But now abideth faith, hope, love, these three; and the greatest of these is love. (ASV)
>
> **1 Corinthians 13:13**

Spiritual Health Assessment ♥
0-1 doesn't match   2-3 partial match   4-5 strong match   x put check mark in the related box

Worship
Each day, loving and learning about God is my highest priority.

0 1 2 3 4 5

Worship
I depend on God for all things in my life.

0 1 2 3 4 5

Worship
I regularly meditate on God's word and invite him into my life and business.

0 1 2 3 4 5

Love Aspects To Focus On ♥   Recommended Reading ♥
Spiritual Health   The Purpose Driven Life

Daily Schedule, Day 1.

AM		PM	
06.00	His Word, First Word, Prayer	12.00	
07.00	Exercise	01.00	
08.00	Pinterest Exercise	02.00	
09.00	Paint Your Vision	03.00	
10.00		04.00	
11.00		05.00	
		06.00	Home with Family
		07.00	
		08.00	His Word, Last Word, Prayer

DISCOVER YOUR PURPOSE

And we know that in all things God works for the good of those who love him, who have been called according to His purpose. (NIV)

Romans 8:28

The idea of discovering and defining your purpose may seem daunting at first. It's one of those abstract concepts, something that seems either intangible to some people or constantly fleeting to others. And that's okay. We are all constantly evolving in our spiritual lives, our personal lives, our careers, and our physical selves. But discovering your purpose is much easier than you think.

The first sentence Pastor Rick Warren writes in his international best-selling book *The Purpose Driven Life* is "It's not about you." But what does "It's not about you" mean to you? "It's not about you" means you are made by God. It means you are made for God. God created you, wired you, timed your birthdate and birthplace, and selected your genetics. God built you, envisioned you, and created you in His own image for a specific divine purpose. But God didn't stop there. He then presented you with an owner's manual—the Bible—and blessed you with the most beautiful gift—the freedom to choose. It is our ability to choose God, to choose stewardship, and to choose love, hope, and faith that makes us truly valuable to our communities, our families, and our planet. Until we understand, accept, and believe that God has blessed us to serve both this world and ourselves to the best of our abilities for His glory and within His divine will for us, life simply will not make much sense.

It is vitally important to understand that you do have a higher purpose, whether you recognize it or not. God made us in His image. Powered by the Holy Spirit, each child of God contains the source for infinite love, infinite spirituality, and infinite compassion. We've all made a wrong turn at one or several points in our lives—but it is learning from those missteps that allows us to grow and understand who we are and what we want. And when we can clearly define who we are, we can discover our purpose.

Your total belief in the word of God is an important factor in understanding your higher purpose. In the same way, by believing in the process you are embarking upon in this book, you are inherently discovering your purpose as an agent.

As we draw closer to God and spend time in Scripture each day, He transforms our hearts. As we go back and reexamine our vision board, it will undoubtedly change over time. For example, many of the material possessions that used to be so important to me no longer matter that much. Today, with my expanding revenue channel, I could start adding Ferraris to my automotive collection. And as much as I like Ferraris, I would not purchase one without seeking God's will through prayers and finding ultimate peace in my decision. In other words, I am able to surrender that particular decision to Him. But if I'm honest with myself, today a Ferrari isn't as exciting to me as it was several years ago. Today, as I'm writing this, I am more excited about allocating the same amount toward an orphanage, seminary, and community church that helps those who are in desperate need of a safe home and medical and mental health attention. This is what is considered God's transformation of the heart.

For where your treasure is, there your heart will be also. (NIV)
Matthew 6:21

Remember, God is actively looking for people to bless. By accepting and knowing that God has promised to care for you and has made a pact with you to lead you toward success, you are using an essential mental tool that will allow you to live and grow in a purpose-driven manner. Doing so will help you serve those around you by first loving God, loving your neighbor, sharing the Good News, and immersing yourself in a life of servitude.

But how do we find our purpose, and how do we ensure that it falls in line with what God has in mind? Here are a few tips to help.

Tips for Discovering Your Purpose

1. Read Scripture.
    Scripture is food for your soul. We must read it daily to remain nourished. Believing in the abundant love God has for you will help you share your love with others, creating a healthy and magnetic environment and opening yourself up to once-hidden opportunities and friendships.

2. Use your missteps to help others.
    It is important to learn from our mistakes. But it is equally important to share those lessons with those around you, bettering the spiritual livelihoods of friends, family, and strangers alike.

3. Be grateful.
    Close your eyes. Take a deep breath. Say one thing that you are grateful for in this moment. Repeat throughout the day.

4. Practice altruism.
    The joy of selflessness creates a chain reaction. When our love and positive energy are transferred between us without ulterior motives, tight societal bonds and relationships are formed, giving your life purpose.

5. Find and participate in a community.

By joining the team at Agentinc., you have surrounded yourself with like-minded people who share similar experiences, successes, fears, and aspirations. Listen to their stories—but most importantly, don't be afraid to tell your own. To continue to learn each day not only from your own actions but also from those around you is an essential element in your personal growth and discovery of purpose.

Some of us may already know our purpose. For others, it may require time and effort. But no matter where you are in your search for purpose right now, know that you will find it—and when you do, you will continue to expand both in your career and in your spirit.

I keep running hard toward the finish line to get the prize that is mine because God has called me through Christ Jesus to life up there in heaven. (ERV)

Philippians 3:14

Spiritual Health Assessment ♥
0-1 doesn't match   2-3 partial match   4-5 strong match   x put check mark in the related box

Worship
I am the same person as an agent that I am in private.

Fellowship
I am an open and honest agent and person.

Fellowship
I use my time and resources to help others, not just in business, but in my personal life.

Love Aspects To Focus On ♥   Recommended Reading ♥
Spiritual Health   The Purpose Driven Life, Chapter 2

Daily Schedule, Day 2.

AM		PM	
06.00	His Word, First Word, Prayer	12.00	
07.00	Exercise	01.00	
08.00	Discover Your Purpose	02.00	
09.00		03.00	
10.00		04.00	
11.00		05.00	
		06.00	Home with Family
		07.00	
		08.00	His Word, Last Word, Prayer

REPAINT YOUR VISION WITH SMART GOALS

Now listen, you who say, "Today or tomorrow we will go to this or that city, spend a year there, carry on business and make money." Why, you do not even know what will happen tomorrow. What is your life? You are a mist that appears for a little while and then vanishes. Instead, you ought to say, "If it is the Lord's will, we will live and do this or that." As it is, you boast in your arrogant schemes. All such boasting is evil. If anyone, then, knows the good they ought to do and doesn't do it, it is sin for them. (NIV)

James 4:13–17

Today is an important day, a day in which you will lay the foundation for your career path moving forward. As a faith-based agent or broker, you may have had thoughts or reservations about how striving for personal financial and career success aligns with the message of God and the teachings found in the Bible. If so, it's important to note that God gave you this planet, this world, your body, your mind, your emotions, your intellect, your love, and your ambition for a reason. We were made by God, and we were made for God, and until we figure this out, nothing about our lives will make much sense. The God who made us is the only one who knows our divine purpose, and we can find our divine purpose in our "Operator's Manual"—the perfect, living, breathing, word of God known as the Scripture, which He gave us to read daily.

Our purpose in life can be summed up in five points:

1. Loving and learning about God (worship)
2. Receiving God's love (discipleship)
3. Caring for those in need (fellowship)
4. Sharing the Good News (mission)
5. Serving others (ministry)

Your decision to bring happiness and comfort to yourself, your family, your children, and your clients conforms with what God intended you to do. It is only when we lose sight of our servitude and our gratitude that our ambition can lead us off the path and undermine what is truly important in our lives.

Remember, life is a test. We are here for 80 years, maybe more or maybe less—and then we are gone.

> Then I turned my thoughts to consider wisdom, and also madness and folly. What more can the king's successor do than what has already been done? I saw that wisdom is better than folly, just as light is better than darkness. The wise have eyes in their heads, while the fool walks in the darkness; but I came to realize that the same fate overtakes them both. Then I said to myself, "The fate of the fool will overtake me also. What then do I gain by being wise?" I said to myself, "This too is meaningless." For the wise, like the fool, will not be long remembered; the days have already come when both have been forgotten. Like the fool, the wise too must die! (NIV)
>
> **Ecclesiastes 2:12–16**

Money and finances are the ultimate acid test. As I mentioned earlier, there are more verses in the Bible about finances than about any other subject. By joyfully giving your money to God, you place Him first.

So, to gain a better understanding of how to achieve our financial and personal goals while still following in the footsteps of Christ, it is important to create and recognize what I like to call "Smart Goals." The basis of Smart Goals is simple. A Smart Goal is a goal blessed by God. If God can't get behind and support your goal, then it's not a Smart Goal.

When you set out to achieve success as a real estate agent, ask yourself if your methods, expectations, and desires are in line with your beliefs and the teachings of Christ. Are the goals you set forth for yourself two days ago products of blind ambition? Are they selfish or sinful? Or are they in line with God's message? A Smart Goal should be based on two things: motive and your willingness to surrender to God. If on day 1, you envisioned yourself in a plush Malibu estate, sipping a cocktail on a yacht, or flying on a PJ to Barbados, that's fine—as long as you put God first, prayed, and surrendered each of those decisions. He may use your estate to hold fundraisers for the needy, use your yacht to entertain donors who can help the church, or use your jet to fly a crew of missionaries to Puerto Rico to help build homes for the homeless. Smart Goals should not be based on satisfying your desires—they should be based on carving out a path toward a greater good for yourself, your community, and the world at large. Remember, whatever your dream is, God has a bigger one. If you put God first in every decision, then it's okay to dream big.

Psalm 72 begins with King David asking God to make his son Solomon the richest, most powerful, and most famous man on earth. On the surface, King David's request sounds selfish. But if we read on, we find out what King David's true motivation behind his request is—to give his son the power, wealth, and fame to help the oppressed. God listened to David and indeed blessed Solomon with great riches. With his riches, King Solomon developed a lavish exotic horse and chariot collection. Today, that collection would be the equivalent of owning a fleet of rare antique cars. It is important to understand that God blessed Solomon with the ability to acquire his collection of horses and chariots because he was dedicated to helping others. Because of Solomon's promise to God, his luxury acquisitions cannot be considered immoral. If we put God first and ask Him to bless us with riches and power so that we may spread love, faith, and hope to the world, then no one should be judged for God's blessing of owning luxury items. Solomon's purpose and motive made the difference. The heart of the matter is a matter of the heart.

"Each year, I set my Smart Goals by looking through a lens of worship, discipleship, fellowship, ministry, and mission, which allows me to define my purpose on the planet while simultaneously achieving my personal and professional expectations."

Personally, I enjoy luxury items—God wired me that way. So setting lofty financial goals has always been vital to my success and vision. Each year, I would lay out ways to increase my business 20 percent so I could travel more, buy more houses and luxury items, and generate a bigger retirement war chest. But over time, I came to realize that these goals were not the reason I was put here on earth. I realized that if all I do is sell a bunch of houses and retire with my treasures, then I will have never realized my true purpose in life.

Now, I shape my future based on Smart Goals. Each year, I set my Smart Goals by looking through a lens of worship, discipleship, fellowship, ministry, and mission, which allows me to define my purpose on the planet while simultaneously achieving my personal and professional expectations. My Smart Goals allow me to place God first and understand success in a more fruitful and loving way. The fulfillment of my Smart Goals provides not only financial freedom but also peace, joy, and eternal rewards. Matthew 6:19–21 states, "Do not store up for yourselves treasures on earth, where moths and vermin destroy, and where thieves break in and steal. But store up for yourselves treasures in heaven, where moths and vermin do not destroy, and where thieves do not break in and steal. For where your treasure is, there your heart will be also." (NIV)

This is my belief. God is the most amazing Creator. He is the best architect, designer, partner, and mentor. We are made in God's image. Therefore, we are most like Him when we are creating. You may have noticed that whenever angels or visions of God are recited in Scripture, those who represent the Lord are generally well dressed, with white and gold sashes and feet made of bronze.

We are built by God to be aspirational. So we are encouraged to like—not love—the brilliant earthly creations God has given us.

As Christian agents, we are blessed to have the ability to elevate the quality of life not only for our clients but also for ourselves, our families, our communities, and our churches. By defining your Smart Goals, you are laying out a blueprint for God and yourself, making it easier for you to identify and achieve what it is you want most out of your career and your faith.

Tips for Discovering Your Own Smart Goals

1. **Be specific.**
   - What do I want to accomplish?
   - Why is this goal important?
2. **Set measurable goals.**
   - What steps do I need to take to accomplish my goals?
   - How will I know when I've accomplished my goals?
3. **Set achievable goals.**
   - How realistic are my goals?
   - Are my goals in line with God's message?
4. **Set relevant goals.**
   If your goals are relevant, the answers to the following questions should be "yes."
   - Are my goals worthwhile to both myself and my community?
   - Am I the right person to reach these goals?
   - Are my goals applicable to the current socioeconomic environment?
5. **Set time-bound goals.**
   - What can I do today to help achieve my goals?
   - Where will I find myself in 40 days when I have completed this book?

As you proceed through this book, be sure to remember why you have made a conscious decision to take this path, and focus on the happiness and comfort you are capable of providing for yourself and your loved ones throughout the journey.

Smart Goal Visualization Exercise (15 minutes)

1. Grab a pen and paper.
2. Find a quiet, peaceful space where you won't be interrupted.
3. Relax and take four large, deep breaths, focusing on inhaling and slowly exhaling.

4. Write down the Smart Goals you wish to accomplish in the next 12 months on your piece of paper.
5. Write one emotion you want to feel 12 months from now. This could be happiness, fulfillment, success, pride, contentment, relaxation, or some other emotion.
6. Look at each of the Smart Goals, one by one, and visualize yourself accomplishing those goals, smiling as you do so. What does the world around you look like when you've successfully achieved these goals? Who is there with you? Where are you? What does it smell like? What do your legs feel like underneath you? What will you eat for dinner that night? Who will you thank?
7. Thank God for providing you with a world filled with an abundance of freedom, opportunity, and love.
8. Place the piece of paper in an envelope, date it, and seal it. Open the envelope one year from today.

Most people overestimate what they can do in a year and they underestimate what they can do in two or three decades.

Tony Robbins

Smart Goals

⚑ WORSHIP
Loving and Learning About God

God has given us life, our minds, our talents, and our bodies to experience joy and happiness, as well as to support our neighbors and better our communities. We are here to fulfill the dreams He has envisioned for us as well as to celebrate the endless beauty and opportunity He has bestowed upon us. By placing God at the center of your life through worship, you eliminate worry, allowing God to be the unbreakable foundation that holds your life together.

DISCIPLESHIP ⚑
Receiving God's Love

We are designed by God to receive and relay the message of love, faith, and hope to everyone we interact with. God expects us to work toward improving ourselves and helping our community by developing an intimate and profound relationship with Christ. We are called to love others just as Jesus loves us. This is a matter of character, and character is built over a lifetime. Who you are as a person is what God values most.

⚑ FELLOWSHIP
Caring for Those in Need

God is love. By helping those in need, we are expressing God's love, exemplifying our Christian commitment to believers, and connecting to God and the family of God here on earth. Our charitable endeavors, as well as our membership and function within our church family, unite us and our community with God.

MISSION ⚑
Sharing the Good News

We are here on earth to share God's love. As agents, we are blessed with the ability to shape clients' futures for generations to come. By committing ourselves to a professional life of stewardship, we are inherently sharing the Good News with believers and unbelievers alike, making a positive impact on our community. Share the lessons you have learned with others and use your testimony to spread the message of Christ.

⚑ MINISTRY
Serving Others

God has promised us not only love, faith, and hope here on earth, but also an eternal life in the Kingdom of Heaven! In exchange for His promises, He asks us to serve others, spread the Good News, and engage in charitable works in His name. By utilizing what Pastor Rick Warren describes as SHAPE (spiritual gifts, heart, abilities, personality, and experiences), you can choose who will benefit most from your service. Remember, your service produces an outpouring of gratitude to God.

Spiritual Health Assessment ♥

0-1 doesn't match   2-3 partial match   4-5 strong match   x put check mark in the related box

Fellowship
There is nothing unresolved in my personal and professional relationships.

`0` `1` `2` `3` `4` `5`

Discipleship
When it comes to finances, I think about God and others more than I do myself.

`0` `1` `2` `3` `4` `5`

Discipleship
God's word advises my business and thoughts.

`0` `1` `2` `3` `4` `5`

Love Aspects To Focus On ♥	Recommended Reading ♥
Spiritual Health	The Purpose Driven Life, Chapter 3

Daily Schedule, Day 3. 🕐

AM		PM	
06.00	His Word, First Word, Prayer	12.00	
07.00	Exercise	01.00	
08.00	Smart Goal Visualization Exercise	02.00	
09.00	Discover Your Smart Goals	03.00	
10.00		04.00	
11.00		05.00	
		06.00	Home with Family
		07.00	
		08.00	His Word, Last Word, Prayer

CONSECRATE YOUR BUSINESS

Again, it will be like a man going on a journey who called his servants and entrusted his wealth to them. To one he gave five bags of gold, to another two bags, and to another one bag, each according to his ability. Then he went on his journey. The man who had received five bags of gold went at once and put his money to work and gained five bags more. So also, the one with two bags of gold gained two more. But the man who had received one bag went off, dug a hole in the ground and hid his master's money.

After a long time the master of those servants returned and settled accounts with them. The man who had received five bags of gold brought the other five. "Master," he said, "you entrusted me with five bags of gold. See, I have gained five more."

His master replied, "Well done, good and faithful servant! You have been faithful with a few things; I will put you in charge of many things. Come and share your master's happiness!"

The man with two bags of gold also came. "Master," he said, "you entrusted me with two bags of gold; see, I have gained two more."

His master replied, "Well done, good and faithful servant! You have been faithful with a few things; I will put you in charge of many things. Come and share your master's happiness!"

Then the man who had received one bag of gold came. "Master," he said, "I knew that you are a hard man, harvesting

24

where you have not sown and gathering where you have not scattered seed. So I was afraid and went out and hid your gold in the ground. See, here is what belongs to you."

His master replied, "You wicked, lazy servant! So you knew that I harvest where I have not sown and gather where I have not scattered seed? Well then, you should have put my money on deposit with the bankers, so that when I returned I would have received it back with interest.

"So take the bag of gold from him and give it to the one who has ten bags. For whoever has will be given more, and they will have an abundance. Whoever does not have, even what they have will be taken from them. And throw that worthless servant outside, into the darkness, where there will be weeping and gnashing of teeth." (NIV)

Matthew 25:14–30

As illustrated in the Parable of the Talents, God expects you to take what you are given and expand upon it. He wants you to take the gifts He has bestowed upon you and turn them into something greater—for yourself and your community. He has blessed you with a wealth of assets. It is up to you to put them to use wisely and without fear. But how can you be sure your decisions are correct? How can you be sure you are running and expanding your business in the most efficient and progressive manner? Perhaps a partner would help. And what if this partner possessed the most powerful and influential mind on earth? And what if this partner expected nothing from you in return aside from a tithe and a commitment of servitude and faith? What if this partner was God?

"How can you be sure you are running and expanding your business in the most efficient and progressive manner?"

Now, if God was your partner, wouldn't you feel better about your career, your business, and your future?

On April 30, 1789, our great nation swore in its first president—George Washington. During his inauguration, Washington consecrated the United States, saying, "It would be peculiarly improper to omit in this first official act my fervent supplications to that Almighty Being Who rules over the universe, Who presides in the councils of nations, and Whose providential aids can supply every human defect—that His benediction may consecrate to the liberties and happiness of the people of the United States a government instituted by themselves for these essential purposes."

No other country on earth has enjoyed the power, global wealth domination, and protection that the United States enjoyed in the years that followed George Washington's consecration of the country. When I started Agentinc., I wanted the same protection and blessing that had allowed America to continue to thrive for centuries. God tells us, "Worry about nothing and pray about everything."

In 1783, six years before he would become president, George Washington developed the Circular to the States, a prayer for our nation. It reads:

I now make it my earnest prayer, that God would have the United States in his holy protection, that he would incline the hearts of the Citizens to cultivate a spirit of subordination and obedience to Government, to entertain a brotherly affection and love for one another, for their fellow citizens of the United States at large, and particularly for their brethren who have served in the field, and finally, that he would most graciously be pleased to dispose us all, to do Justice, to love mercy, and to demean ourselves with that Charity, humility and pacific temper of mind, which were the Characteristics of the Devine Author of our blessed Religion, and without an humble imitation of whose example in these things, we can never hope to be a happy Nation.

Throughout the Old Testament and throughout all of history, there have been chosen nations that at times either turned to God and received His blessings or turned away from God and received the exact opposite. On the day George Washington consecrated our country, he took the first step in creating the most influential and successful nation in the world—and he did it with God as his partner.

The truth is, God is ready and willing to be your partner as well. He is willing to walk alongside you each step of the way. He is willing to bring you and your family and your loved ones joy, happiness, and peace. He is willing to pay the rent, the mortgage, and the electric bill.

But a successful business partnership is based on communication. In order for God to accept a partnership with you, you must allow Him to listen to your concerns, fears, and triumphs. You must grant Him access to every aspect of your business and your life. You must be truly honest with Him. You must look to Him for advice, and you must trust His message and His guidance.

By giving God the keys to your business, you are taking the stress off your shoulders and putting your faith and trust in a proven partner—He's never failed! But remember, every partnership is a two-way street. If you allow God to take on the responsibility of helping you build your business, then you must listen to His message, talk with Him, pray to Him, and reward Him with the glory and spiritual profits of His investment in you.

Now is the time to reflect on your commitment to your career and to God. Take this day to ask God to be your business partner and to celebrate your union with Him. Draw up a business plan and a sales agreement with God, stating that you are selling a majority stake in your business to Him, allowing Him to become the primary shareholder. In exchange for His blessing and guidance, provide 10 percent of your income to Him through tithing, and keep Him duly informed of your progress along the way. Understand this—God is a willing chairman, unlike any other, who has the expertise, knowledge, and power to accomplish anything, and He is willing to work for a minimal amount of what you earn.

By creating a business relationship with God, you are consciously allowing your faith to take part in your financial future. If you truly believe in the beauty, righteousness, and light that God brings to you on a spiritual level, then shouldn't it feel just as good to allow Him to bless your career and finances with that same wisdom and light? Allowing God to access your entire being—be it spiritually, financially, or personally—welcomes positivity and growth that translates to success, contentment, and joy.

It is essential to understand that when we plan, create, and build while placing God first, we can successfully realize His vision of success. But if we plan, create, and build in defiance of God, we cannot expect to be blessed. The matter at hand is a matter of the heart. Utilize these 40 days of farming to not only plan and build toward your glorious harvest but also to allow God to begin the transformation in your heart.

Business Consecration

On this day, Heavenly Father, I proclaim my purpose in establishing Agentinc., to which You have called me. I promise to glorify You each day and to surrender my will to You in the hope that You will guide me on the path toward righteousness and service. I promise to use the talents, the wisdom, and the knowledge You have bestowed upon me to create and expand Agentinc. in Your image. I offer up my hands to You for Your purpose, that I might continue to spread the Good News to those I have the opportunity to work with.

I promise, loving God, to pray to You, to include You in every decision I make, to come to You when I need advice and guidance, and to use the love, faith, and hope powered by Your Holy Spirit to enhance the lives of my clients, my associates, and my fellow agents. I promise, Most High, to please You first in all my endeavors and to hold on to my faith and place it in the over 7,000 promises You have made in Scripture. Within those promises, I willingly accept the assurance of "Shalom," the blessing Lord Jesus Christ bestowed upon His disciples following His resurrection, and understand that Your intention is to provide me with the immense gifts contained within Shalom—safety, rest, prosperity, wholeness, welfare, completion, fullness, soundness, and well-being for eternity. In addition, I agree to uphold the Sabbath and dedicate one day each week to worship as well as rest, so that I may both praise You and enjoy the world You have blessed us with.

Almighty Creator, I praise You for the entrepreneurial spirit You have given me. With Agentinc.'s each achievement, I will honor You by tithing 40 percent of our earnings to continue Your mission and spread Your message of love. Give me the courage to build a solid and unfaltering foundation for Agentinc. based on Your truth and Your standards.

Lord, I consecrate Agentinc. in Your name, so that I might use my hands, my mind, and my heart to service others to the best of my ability. I ask You to be my partner, to lead me toward my ultimate goals in the Kingdom of Heaven, and to support me eternally throughout my life, professionally and spiritually.

Amen!

Spiritual Health Assessment ♥
0-1 doesn't match   2-3 partial match   4-5 strong match   x put check mark in the related box

Discipleship
I praise God during difficult times and learn from my adversity.

Discipleship
My decisions as an agent are modeled after the teachings of Jesus.

Love Aspects To Focus On ♥   Recommended Reading ♥
Spiritual Health   The Purpose Driven Life, Chapter 4

Daily Schedule, Day 4. 🕐

AM	PM
06.00 His Word, First Word, Prayer	12.00
07.00 Exercise	01.00
08.00 Meditate on the Concept of God as Your Partner	02.00
	03.00
09.00	04.00
10.00	05.00
11.00 Consecrate Your Business	06.00 Home with Family
	07.00
	08.00 His Word, Last Word, Prayer

JOIN THE RIGHT AGENCY

Two are better than one, because they have a good reward for their toil. For if they fall, one will lift up his fellow. But woe to him who is alone when he falls and has not another to lift him up! Again, if two lie together, they keep warm, but how can one keep warm alone? And though a man might prevail against one who is alone, two will withstand him—a threefold cord is not quickly broken. (ESV)

Ecclesiastes 4:9–12

Now that you've clearly identified your goals and ambitions both in your real estate and personal endeavors, it's time to find the perfect agency!

Finding the agency that meets your lifestyle demands and financial expectations can be difficult, and many agents have a hard time finding an agency that truly works for them. In the case of Agentinc., I built a real estate brokerage company founded on the core value of being agent-centric. Agentinc. was built *by* agents, *for* agents, to help agents become more successful, and has ancillary companies in place to ensure that your needs are met across the entire realm of real estate. Being part of the Agentinc. team means more than just working for an up-and-coming brand—we value our relationships and encourage our agents to work together to generate success for the entire Agentinc. team. As John Wooden said, "The main ingredient of stardom is the team." Your decision to join any agency, including Agentinc., means you have surrounded yourself with like-minded individuals with similar goals and values. You have taken a step, just like your fellow agents, to build a better future founded upon not just selling houses but working together to generate income and increase visibility.

At Agentinc., we are proud of the differentiators that have made us one of the fastest-growing real estate companies in the country:

Revenue Share Program
Luxury marketing
Buy a Neighborhood Program
Sponsored digital marketing
Build your own publication
State-of-the-art resource center
Ground-floor opportunity/global ambition
Planned future stock ownership

Agentinc. is the only agency out there that provides agents with advanced technology, innovative marketing strategies, and vendor support programs designed to help them build their clientele and succeed in a competitive market.

As you can tell by the title of this book, Agentinc. is deeply committed to and focused on the practice of farming through our Buy a Neighborhood Program, as well as to promoting you as a neighborhood specialist, both of which help you become immediately recognizable in your farm.

With our progressive Revenue Share Program, we allow you to gather passive income by referring associates to Agentinc., ensuring that you earn money between listings and expand your reach domestically and globally.

At Agentinc., we believe it is possible to achieve our personal, spiritual, and financial goals while remaining true to our beliefs and our core values. Together, we have the power and ability to shape our clients' futures and our own futures. By joining the Agentinc. team, you are contributing to not only your own success but also that of your clients and your fellow associates, who rely on your professionalism and talent to elevate our business.

Agentinc. expects all agents to adhere to our core values:

Exceptional service
Consummate professionalism
Integrity
Purposeful cooperation
Accountability
Professional code of ethics

On day 5, it is important to review all your agency materials, begin or complete a New Agent Checklist, and reach out to your company with any questions you may have.

Tomorrow, the journey continues. But for today, know that no matter who you've decided to work with, you are now part of a real estate company that believes in your abilities as an agent and has given you the opportunity to build your business and brand.

New Agent Checklist

✓ Obtain your e-license with Agent License (change your employing broker to Agentinc. DRE# 02068079).

✓ Complete your board forms (transfer or board application).

✓ Pay your E&O insurance for the year.

✓ Attend a new agent orientation.

✓ Order business cards.

✓ Order signs ("Open House" and "For Sale").

✓ Create your email signature.

✓ View the listing presentation.

✓ Have your headshot taken.

✓ Write your bio.

✓ Choose your farm, register with your local broker, and post hashtagged photos of your neighborhood (e.g., #CameoShores).

✓ For Agentinc. Agents:
  • Log into the Agentinc. dashboard.
  • Select a digital suite membership.

Spiritual Health Assessment ♥

0-1 doesn't match   2-3 partial match   4-5 strong match   x put check mark in the related box

Ministry
I regularly use my time to serve God.

`0` ☐ `1` ☐ `2` ☐ `3` ☐ `4` ☐ `5` ☐

Ministry
I serve God by using the talents he has given me to expand our business.

`0` ☐ `1` ☐ `2` ☐ `3` ☐ `4` ☐ `5` ☐

Love Aspects To Focus On ♥   Recommended Reading ♥
Spiritual Health   The Purpose Driven Life, Chapter 5

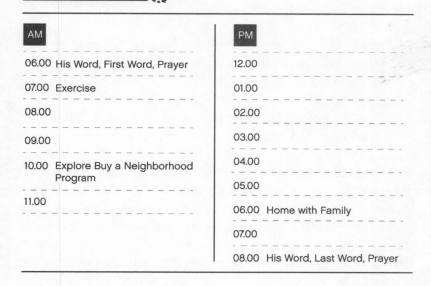

Daily Schedule, Day 5.

AM		PM	
06.00	His Word, First Word, Prayer	12.00	
07.00	Exercise	01.00	
08.00		02.00	
09.00		03.00	
10.00	Explore Buy a Neighborhood Program	04.00	
11.00		05.00	
		06.00	Home with Family
		07.00	
		08.00	His Word, Last Word, Prayer

Day 6

GET A PROFESSIONAL HEADSHOT

As in water face reflects face, so the heart of man reflects man. (AMP)

Proverbs 27:19

Visualization is a two-way street for both agent and client. Just as you have been adding images of the future to your Pinterest board and connecting with the physical manifestations of your future, your clients have been engaging in a similar process.

If you've ever been through the process of buying or selling your home, you know that you have certain expectations and hopes. If you're looking to purchase a home, you envision the garden, the mountain view, the summer breeze flowing through the open windows, the dinners you'll prepare for your family and friends, Christmas mornings, Fourth of July celebrations—and then, one day, you're in that home, celebrating these events just as you envisioned them. If you're selling, you see your next home, your next city, your next adventure, the money deposited into your savings account, the boat you always wanted to buy—and then, with the help of an agent, these goals are realized.

Your headshot is the first step in a client's actualization of these visions. They know that in order to make one of the biggest decisions of their lives, they need the guidance and expertise of an agent willing to go the extra mile for them. They know that they need an agent who is positive, who is a joy to be around, who is professional, and who is committed to their craft. Your headshot is the first impression your client will have of you—it reflects your heart. They will look at your picture and ask themselves, "Do I see a professional? Is this the person who will help me realize my future goals?"

When I started in the real estate business, I had very little money. But I knew that the way I would be perceived by the public was very important. I saved up my money and went to Figge Photography, the most expensive studio in Orange County, and they captured a shot of me that I used consistently for a decade. My arms were crossed, my smile was genuine, and I wore a jacket with no tie to seem approachable yet professional. This photo was seen millions of times. Today we call this "impressions"—the amount of times people view a photo. It was well worth the money, and its familiarity helped people recognize and remember me as I built my business. The more people see of your torso, the more comfortable they feel with you.

Take a moment to look at yourself in the mirror. Take a deep breath. Relax and close your eyes. Imagine yourself selling your first home for a client as an agent. Imagine the joy you feel as a result of your success and the joy your client feels in their accomplishment. Smile and let these emotions and excitement take hold of your entire being. Now, open your eyes. This is the agent people want to work with.

"First impressions count, not only in real estate but also throughout life."

You may be asking yourself, "Why do I need a professional photographer? My iPhone camera is amazing." The simple fact is, there is a reason why professional photographers exist—because they make you look like the agent people want to work with. So instead of placing your iPhone on a window ledge and setting the timer for 10 seconds, follow these steps to ensure a perfect headshot:

1. **Hire a professional photographer who specializes in headshots.**

   We all have a friend who is either an "amateur photographer" or owns "a great camera," or whose hobby is "photography." These are not the people to call on when it is time to take a professional headshot for your business. Again, professionals are professionals for a reason. They will adjust the lighting and tell you where to look, how to align your profile, where to place your hands, how to breathe, and how to smile. The result—a compelling photograph that reflects your heart and your commitment to professionalism.

2. **Dress successfully.**

   We are all created equal in God's eyes. But for a client, agents who respect their appearance elicit respect. By dressing successfully, you are telling the visual story to the world that you have the drive and determination to bring positive change to your clients. You are telling your clients that you take their business seriously. It's important to note that dressing "successfully" doesn't mean everyone has to look the same. Choose an outfit that both expresses your personality and maintains the high level of respect you want to portray to your clients and to your colleagues. Remember, not all clients have the same ideals, religion, politics, beliefs, and musical tastes as you do. What you wear reflects who you are inside. First impressions count, not only in real estate but also throughout life.

3. **Don't be shy. Have fun!**

   Some people were born to be in front of the camera. Others shy away from the lens. It's important to feel comfortable in your own skin. The camera captures emotions. When we are angry or stressed or tired or worried or unconfident, our faces reflect exactly what is happening inside. Conversely, when we are happy, relaxed, hopeful, and carefree, we exude a level of confidence and positivity that is recognizable from the corners of our lips, to the apex of our eyes, around our jaw muscles, and up into our foreheads. If you embrace this moment of putting yourself out into the world and fill yourself with gratitude for allowing God to guide you on a path to better your life and your clients' lives, your clients will be able to see who you are and what your heart is reflecting.

Spiritual Health Assessment ♥
0-1 doesn't match   2-3 partial match   4-5 strong match   x put check mark in the related box

Ministry
Friends, colleagues, and fellow agents would say I enjoy giving more than receiving.

☐0 ☐1 ☐2 ☐3 ☐4 ☐5

Evangelism
I look to build relationships with those who don't know Jesus.

☐0 ☐1 ☐2 ☐3 ☐4 ☐5

Love Aspects To Focus On ♥   Recommended Reading ♥
Spiritual Health   The Purpose Driven Life, Chapter 6

Daily Schedule, Day 6. 🕐

AM	PM
06.00 His Word, First Word, Prayer	12.00
07.00 Exercise	01.00
08.00 Prepare for Your Photograph	02.00
09.00 Take Your Photograph	03.00
10.00	04.00
11.00	05.00
	06.00 Home with Family
	07.00
	08.00 His Word, Last Word, Prayer

SELECT YOUR FARM AND COLLECT FARM DATA

"And if you will indeed obey my commandments that I command you today, to love the Lord your God, and to serve him with all your heart and with all your soul, he will give the rain for your land in its season, the early rain and the later rain, that you may gather in your grain and your wine and your oil. And he will give grass in your fields for your livestock, and you shall eat and be full." (ESV)

Deuteronomy 11:13–15

Welcome to day 7, one of the most important and influential days of your 40-day journey toward personal, spiritual, and professional enlightenment and success. It's time to select your farm!

Real estate coaching and training expert Tom Ferry says, "The realization of your plan is worth more than any single transaction. Refuse to let your business interfere with your plan. Trust the process." In other words, if a potential buyer wants to drag you around in an adjacent county on weekends, refer the business. Don't let this happen to you. Selecting your farm is one of the biggest business decisions you will make in your career. It is incredibly important to be thoughtful and aware of your time and skills when making this decision, and as you move forward, it is equally important to trust the process. There are a number of factors you should consider when deciding where, geographically, you would like to dedicate your time, energy, and presence when it comes to farming. There are three important guidelines that should heavily influence your decision:

1. Select a neighborhood you currently reside in or would like to reside in.
2. Select an area you are passionate about.
3. Find a neighborhood with at least 1,000 homes, or three contiguous neighborhoods that equal 1,000 homes.

Let's start with selecting a neighborhood you currently reside in or would like to reside in. Because gaining visibility within your farm is of the utmost importance, and because you will be spending most of your time developing relationships within a particular area, it is logical that working inside a community you are already part of (or wish to someday become part of) would be a wise step. The neighborhood where you live offers a nearly 24-hour opportunity to expand your network. There are restaurants, grocery stores, salons, retail shops, sidewalks, gas stations, hotels, playgrounds, and schools—all filled with potential clients with whom you have something in common.

"To become a neighborhood specialist, you must
be passionate about the amenities, however
small or large, your farm possesses."

Think of your community as much more than a group of people who simply share the same zip code. Your community, just like the Christian community, is built on a framework of companionship and loyalty. We may not be defined spiritually by where we live, but we are a part of something larger—a geographic location that provides food, shelter, entertainment, and most of all, friendships to ourselves, our loved ones, and our families. And remember, your proximity to your farm is an essential aspect of managing your time efficiently. By selecting a geographically convenient farm area, you can reduce commuting time, as well as eliminate the need to chase clients across several zip codes, which can diminish your visibility and break your momentum.

Next, it is important to be passionate about where you farm. As we discussed a few days ago, discovering your purpose and visualizing your goals as an agent are important steps toward realizing your future success. In order to achieve this success, it is incredibly important to choose an area you feel particularly connected to, that you are particularly proud of, and that represents the kinds of homes, people, and lifestyles you feel are best suited to your skill set. But let's be realistic—we can't all live on Lido Isle or in Bel-Air. That's why it's important to select a neighborhood where you genuinely want to spend a majority of your time.

At Agentinc., we encourage our agents to exclusively claim a neighborhood and become a neighborhood specialist. But in order to become a neighborhood specialist, you must dedicate yourself to knowing every detail about your farm. To become a neighborhood specialist, you must be passionate about the amenities, however small or large, your farm possesses. To become a neighborhood specialist, you must make your presence known in the community, you must be proud to support the people and the businesses within it, you must be willing to serve the community outside your real estate endeavors, and most of all, you must always make a concerted effort to be visible within it.

Lastly, your farm should contain at least 1,000 homes. Get to know these 1,000 homes and their residents. Make it your passion to study the architecture, to know the best schools, to frequent the finest (and not so finest) dining establishments. Find a common bond with the residents of these 1,000 homes. As we discussed earlier, being a real estate agent means more than selling homes—it is an act of servitude. That is why it is important to distinguish yourself as someone who is dedicated to helping everyone in your area with all aspects of real estate, as well as life.

If you've decided to become an Agentinc. agent, once you have carefully selected your farm it's important to decide which Agentinc. technology package is best suited to your demands and aspirations.

By devoting yourself to the betterment of your farm, you are serving your community and allowing God to provide you with the necessary means to "eat and be full."

Spiritual Health Assessment ♥

0-1 doesn't match   2-3 partial match   4-5 strong match   x put check mark in the related box

Evangelism

I am confident and comfortable in sharing my faith.

| 0 | | 1 | | 2 | | 3 | | 4 | | 5 | |

Evangelism

I am open to all opportunities when it comes to sharing my faith, and do so with respect and love toward others.

| 0 | | 1 | | 2 | | 3 | | 4 | | 5 | |

Love Aspects To Focus On ♥	Recommended Reading ♥
Spiritual Health	The Purpose Driven Life, Chapter 7

Daily Schedule, Day 7. 🕐

AM	PM
06.00 His Word, First Word, Prayer	12.00
07.00 Exercise	01.00
08.00 Select Your Farm	02.00
09.00	03.00
10.00	04.00
11.00 Collect Farm Data	05.00
	06.00 Home with Family
	07.00
	08.00 His Word, Last Word, Prayer

SELECT YOUR DIGITAL SUITE MEMBERSHIP LEVEL/UTILIZE YOUR COMPANY'S PLATFORM

Sow your seed in the morning, and at evening let your hands not be idle, for you do not know which will succeed, whether this or that, or whether both will do equally well. (NIV)

Ecclesiastes 11:6

N ow that you are ready to launch your business, it's time to focus on generating a client base. God wants us to communicate with each other, to befriend each other, to love each other as He loves us. Nowadays, it has become easier and easier for us all to connect and provide our services to one another. But how do we build a community of friends and clients that we can serve directly as both agents and stewards? At Agentinc., the process is simple. But no matter which brokerage you work with, you'll be able to leverage their tools to help expand your brand.

For Agentinc. agents: First, launch the Agentinc. app! The Agentinc. app is an easy to use, effective tool we give our agents— and it allows you to access all our information anywhere.

Second, one of the most important steps you can take to increase engagement and reach out to your farm is creating and organizing a CRM (customer relationship management technology) by selecting your Agentinc. digital suite membership and purchasing the email addresses and phone numbers in your farm through a respected source like ReboGateway. Our industry is competitive. Every agent is looking to connect with potential clients and turn a lead into a sale or a purchase. Because of the increasing competitiveness of our industry, it is absolutely essential to reach out to more prospective clients than you are physically capable of reaching, to befriend them, and to offer services through a filter of love.

It's true—creating an impressive CRM from a crowded database takes dedication and organization. Not only that, but after you generate leads, you must contact each lead individually and maintain an open line of communication. This sounds like a ton of time-consuming work, and normally it is—which is why many new agents completely ignore this step. However, creating a CRM and digital drip campaign with Agentinc. is easier than you think. Agentinc.'s AI Touch program allows you to create engaging email drip campaigns designed to generate leads by scheduling first, second, and third touches to all contacts in your CRM with approved branded messaging, keeping you in touch within your sphere of influence and allowing you to manage your time efficiently while prioritizing your schedule.

"If you aim to be competitive and successful in your career and stewardship as an agent, it is important to learn and utilize AI Touch to successfully manage time and begin building your clientele list."

I can honestly tell you from personal experience that it is exponentially gratifying to wake up in the morning to find several prospective client responses to a drip campaign I've created on the AI Touch software. It's even more gratifying to know that I was able to generate these leads and financial opportunities without having to spend endless hours on the phone or in front of my computer. If you aim to be competitive and successful in your career and stewardship as an agent, it is important to learn and utilize AI Touch to successfully manage time and begin building your clientele list.

Here are a few notes on how to create an effective CRM and drip campaign with the AI Touch system:

1. Obtain contacts and group them accordingly.
2. Import your contacts.
3. Organize your automated campaign.
4. Schedule your automated follow-up campaign.

Remember, God is always watching us when it comes to how we effectively use the gifts He has given us. Taking the time to understand and appreciate your craft will allow you to optimize your potential spiritually, mentally, and financially.

MENU	ONYX	BRONZE	SILVER	GOLD	PLATINUM
Personalized Agent inc. email address	✓	✓	✓	✓	✓
Personalized landing page	✓ i	✓ i	✓ i	✓ i	✓ i
Mobile Search App	✓ i	✓ i	✓ i	✓ i	✓ i
Neighborhood Specialist Social Media Ads	✓ i	✓ i	✓ i	✓ i	✓ i
Organic Leads from Agentinc.co	✓ i	✓ i	✓ i	✓ i	✓ i
Microsoft Office Suite + Agent inc. Email		✓ i	✓ i	✓ i	✓ i
Ai Touch CMS		✓ i	✓ i	✓ i	✓ i
Personalized Mobile Search App		✓ i	✓ i	✓ i	✓ i
Agent Website essentials		✓ i	✓ i	✓ i	✓ i
ReboGateway	NEW Nationwide Access Account			✓ i	✓ i	✓ i
Just Listed Social Media Ads			✓ i	✓ i	✓ i
Open House Social Media Ads			✓ i	✓ i	✓ i
Just Sold Social Media Ads			✓ i	✓ i	✓ i
Agent Personal Website Pro				✓ i	✓ i
Online Retargeting and Lead Generation				✓ i	✓ i
Social Media Management					✓ i
Digital Marketing Report					✓ i
Customized Marketing Campaign					✓ i
Blog Posting to Social Media					✓ i
Agent Elevated **SmartBooth**					✓ i
	$99/m Gratis	$249/m $99/mo	$449/m $249/mo	$994/m $449/mo	$3495/m $1699/mo
		JOIN	JOIN	JOIN	JOIN

Download Agent Inc.

Agent Inc. is available now for your smartphone or tablet.

Download on the **App Store**　　GET IT ON **Google Play**

Physical Health Assessment ♥
0-1 doesn't match   2-3 partial match   4-5 strong match   x put check mark in the related box

I regularly exercise or take part in healthy activities.

| 0 | | 1 | | 2 | | 3 | | 4 | | 5 | |

I eat healthy as much as possible.

| 0 | | 1 | | 2 | | 3 | | 4 | | 5 | |

Love Aspects To Focus On ♥   Recommended Reading ♥
Physical Health   The TB12 Method

Daily Schedule, Day 8. 🕐

AM		PM	
06.00	His Word, First Word, Prayer	12.00	
07.00	Exercise	01.00	
08.00	Review AI Touch System	02.00	
09.00	Onboard CRM and Agent Inc. App	03.00	
		04.00	
10.00	Set Up AI Touch Contacts and Automated Campaigns	05.00	
11.00		06.00	Home with Family
		07.00	
		08.00	His Word, Last Word, Prayer

DEFINE YOUR VALUE PROPOSITION

"For I know the plans I have for you," declares the Lord, "plans to prosper you and not to harm you, plans to give you hope and a future." (NIV)

Jeremiah 29:11

Welcome to day 9! Hopefully you are settling into your life as an agent and finding a daily balance of spirituality, physical health, and proactivity. By now, I hope you're beginning to understand that God has a dream for you much larger than anything you can possibly dream up yourself. He wants to give you prosperity. He wants to give you hope and a future. He wants you to have a purpose. You are here on earth to provide happiness and comfort to yourself, your family, and your loved ones. Your success brings joy not only to yourself and your spirit but also to the clients you help on their own paths to success.

But in order to generate success and realize your full potential in real estate, it is important to distinguish yourself as an agent who possesses the knowledge and stewardship needed to help those around you achieve their real estate goals. To distinguish

yourself as the ideal agent for your clients, it is essential to define
your value proposition.

But what is a value proposition? A value proposition is a concise
and compelling description of the core benefit people receive when
they work with you. Ask yourself these questions: What do I have
to offer that people can't get from anyone else? What problems can I
solve for my clients that no one else can? What personal services do
I provide for clients that are superior to other agents' services? How
will people remember who I am? How will people find me?

When I was first starting out in real estate in the exclusive,
highly competitive market of Lido Isle in Newport Beach, I realized
right out of the gate that I needed to separate myself from everyone
else—otherwise, I wouldn't have a chance. Cellular phones had just
become a staple tool of real estate back then, and I took some time
to think of how this new technology could help me reach the residents in my farm and expand my brand and name.

With the help of a graphic designer, I created flyers for my farm
that included a picture of a cell phone and a note that read "I'll call
you back within 90 seconds, guaranteed" and blanketed Lido Isle
with my new marketing materials. Guess what happened—people
started calling me. They knew that in 90 seconds they could have
a discussion with an agent about their real estate endeavors. They
knew someone would be on the other end of their phone in only
90 seconds to answer questions with kindness, service, and knowledge. It got to a point where I had people calling me at all hours of
the night and in church on Sundays—just to see if I would pick up.
And I did, every single time. And that's how I became known as
"the 90-Second Man."

"They knew that in 90 seconds, they could have a discussion
with an agent about their real estate endeavors."

My ability to distinguish myself early on in my career has led directly to my success today. I was dedicated to placing myself at the forefront of the conversation when it came to the subject of real estate on Lido Isle. As the calls came pouring in, the deals began closing.

But how can you define your own value proposition? Here are a few pointers to help get you started:

1. **Define what makes you an asset.**
   Is it your unparalleled knowledge of the amenities in your farm? Is it your ability to connect with others on common ground? Is it your previous numbers and real estate awards? Is it your listening skills? Is it your ability to speak several languages? Is it your around-the-clock availability?

   It's important to know that you are an asset not only to your family, to the brand, and to the planet, but also to God. Use your gifts, however small you think they may be, to set yourself apart.

2. **Be clear and concise about what you offer.**
   When grabbing the attention of potential clients, it's essential to keep it simple yet catchy. Focus on one or two of your strengths and/or services and present them in a well-defined manner.

3. **Know your competitors.**
   In order to find your own value proposition, you must first know what everyone else out there is offering. Is what you offer different? Is what you offer better? Find something that no one else is doing your way, and do it.

4. **Solve a problem.**
   One of the best ways to grab prospective clients' attention is to identify a problem everyone in your farm may have in common and find a way to address it. Now, you may not be able to change the traffic, noise, or quality of schools in your farm—but you may be able to find a way to ease concerns

and offer alternatives. Putting in the effort to alleviate the difficulties in your community goes a long way as far as lasting impressions are concerned.

5. **Stand out.**

Once you've found what distinguishes you from the rest of the pack, get your message out there by investing in marketing materials that elevate your brand and presence in your farm. Work with graphic designers, copywriters, or even utilize Agentinc.'s own in-house marketing team to bring your value proposition to life.

Physical Health Assessment ♥
0-1 doesn't match   2-3 partial match   4-5 strong match   x put check mark in the related box

I am proud of the body God has given me.

`0` `1` `2` `3` `4` `5`

I feel physically capable of taking on the tasks required to be a successful agent.

`0` `1` `2` `3` `4` `5`

Love Aspects To Focus On ♥   Recommended Reading ♥
Physical Health   The TB12 Method

Daily Schedule, Day 9. 🕐

AM		PM	
06.00	His Word, First Word, Prayer	12.00	
07.00	Exercise	01.00	Establish Your Value Proposition
08.00	Define What Makes You an Asset	02.00	
09.00	Research Competitors	03.00	
10.00		04.00	
11.00		05.00	
		06.00	Home with Family
		07.00	
		08.00	His Word, Last Word, Prayer

DETERMINE YOUR DIFFERENTIATORS

For we are his workmanship, created in Christ Jesus for good works, which God prepared beforehand, that we should walk in them. (ESV)

Ephesians 2:10

It's time to keep the ball rolling! Today we are selling "you." Today is your elevator pitch. We're going to expand on your value proposition to determine your own differentiators outside of Agentinc. or your chosen brokerage. Once you've established your differentiators, you'll be able to seamlessly integrate these talking points into your bio, marketing materials, email blasts, and quick pitches to prospective clients and strangers in your farm.

If you've already established your value proposition (or at least have been ruminating on it), then you've most likely been able to focus on a few aspects of your personality, experience, education, and knowledge that set you apart from your competition. Understanding the subtle differences between you and fellow agents can propel you forward and expand your network. But in order to continue to expand, you must build your brand.

When building a brand, it is important to hone in and focus on your strengths. Do you have more experience than others? Are you young and just starting out, filled with energy and able to run circles around the competition? Are you the first one in and the last one out? Do you provide wisdom and patience?

We are God's workmanship. We were all created with a vast array of talents that make us unique and give us the power to love. Sometimes, it's difficult to see the gifts God has given us because we aren't always looking within ourselves—we get stuck on what we see with our eyes. We get bogged down with how we've defined ourselves for our entire lives. But these definitions can change when we search for and find those hidden gifts, no matter how big or small, that give us the ability to become successful spiritually and financially.

To help define your differentiators, let's start with an exercise.

First, write down five strengths that you bring to real estate:

1.
2.
3.
4.
5.

Next, research other agents in and around your farm. Look at their bios, the clients they represent, and the styles and prices of homes they bring to the market. Write down a few of their strengths:

1.
2.
3.
4.
5.

Look at your two lists. Are any of your strengths different from the other agents' strengths? If any of them are, you've found your differentiators.

When it comes to an effective marketing strategy, you must first identify your demographic and then produce content geared to engage and connect with the people in your farm. In order to create an effective marketing strategy that highlights your differentiators, start out by researching the average age of your farm. Find out how long residents commute to and from work. Gain an understanding of what their income is. Gather neighborhood statistics. Once you've obtained a firm grasp on what makes up your client base, ask yourself which of your strengths you can promote to elicit a response from your demographic, and then incorporate this information into your bio and marketing materials.

As we discussed yesterday, setting yourself apart from your fellow agents and generating a presence in your farm is essential to creating momentum in your career. We are all blessed with numerous strengths that far outweigh our weaknesses. It may be difficult to grasp all your strengths on any given day, but just remember, God created us in His image. Utilize those gifts now to connect with your future clients.

Physical Health Assessment ♥

0-1 doesn't match   2-3 partial match   4-5 strong match   x put check mark in the related box

I engage in doctor physicals each year.

`0` `1` `2` `3` `4` `5`

I encourage loved ones to maintain a healthy diet.

`0` `1` `2` `3` `4` `5`

Love Aspects To Focus On ♥   Recommended Reading ♥
Physical Health   The TB12 Method

Daily Schedule, Day 10. 🕐

AM		PM	
06.00	His Word, First Word, Prayer	12.00	
07.00	Exercise	01.00	Hone Your Personal Marketing Strategy
08.00	Differentiators Exercises	02.00	
09.00		03.00	
10.00		04.00	
11.00	Gather Data on Farm	05.00	
		06.00	Home with Family
		07.00	
		08.00	His Word, Last Word, Prayer

CREATE A TAGLINE

My heart overflows with a good theme; I address my verses to
the King; My tongue is the pen of a ready writer. (NASB)

Psalm 45:1

By now, you should be starting to realize you are more than just
an agent—you are your own brand. And as a brand, you need
to focus on what it is you represent to the marketplace and to the
industry. You must communicate a message that not only engages
people with love and gratitude but also grants them access to you.
In order for them to recognize and seek out your services, you need
to instill a memory. And one of the strongest ways to convey your
message, generate a memory, and grant prospective clients access
to your skill set is by creating a strong, yet simple, tagline.

Your tagline is a powerful recognition tool. It will define who
you are across your farm. It will be on business cards, mailers, websites, and all social media platforms. Your tagline will most likely
be the first verbal communication you have with a client. This is
why it is vital to choose strong, visual words that convey your
experience, your expertise, and your dedication to your craft.

Last week, you found and explored your differentiators. These
qualities should make up the core messaging of your tagline. When

creating your tag, revisit what it is that makes you different, as well as the character traits that give you an advantage. Remember, let your heart overflow with "a good theme."

Here's a quick checklist of what to do to create a catchy tagline that resonates with your clients.

1. **Research top agent taglines.**
   Learn from the best and you will be the best. Search agents you admire or who put up the best numbers in your farm, and read their taglines. Do you see a common thread among them? Are the words they choose powerful? Do they flow off the tongue? Do they evoke an image? Do they convey professionalism, experience, and expertise?

2. **Ask yourself, What are the clients in my farm afraid of?**
   This is a simple case of problem/solution. If the majority of homeowners and homebuyers in your farm share a common problem, create a tag that addresses that problem and solves it.

"The more taglines you generate, the easier it will become to find something that encompasses your messaging in a simple, catchy, and direct manner."

---

3. **Ask yourself, What are some of the best compliments I have received or other agents in my farm have received?**
   By understanding and identifying what makes the residents in your farm happy, you will be able to successfully create a tag that appeals directly to everything they value in an agent. If it is your around-the-clock service that impresses a majority of clients, it may be wise to incorporate that messaging into your tagline.

4. **Keep it simple.**

    When coming up with a tagline, many people tend to try to cram all their good qualities into one sentence. Instead, keep your demographic in mind and select one or two of your differentiators that suit your farm best.

5. **Start writing.**

    With taglines, practice makes perfect. The more taglines you generate, the easier it will become to find something that encompasses your messaging in a simple, catchy, and direct manner. Write down 10 today, 2 tomorrow, 20 on Saturday. Ask your friends and family if anything sticks out. Take a vote. But most of all, don't expect your tagline to come to you right away like a message from the angel Gabriel. Like everything you have done thus far in your life, making the right decision takes time, practice, success, and even a little bit of failure.

    Once you've created a tagline for your brand, take a moment to make sure it tells the story you want to convey to the world. It may take time (and even a few changes), but once you've selected the right wording, you'll be able to more easily connect with your farm, making an impression on your future clients and generating a subconscious connection. By now, you may be feeling like you've been dedicating all your time to your career. But remember, it is also very important to take some time to care for yourself physically and mentally. Experience something different. Exercise. Try a new food. Watch a film you might not normally watch. Read a book. Anything that breaks up the day-to-day activity of launching your career will allow your brain much-needed rest and will provide the inspiration and additional stamina required to successfully establish yourself.

DEBORAH ROBINSON
EXCEPTIONAL . UNIQUE . GLOBAL

MANOUCHERI
PASSION FOR EXCELLENCE

SHAWN HALAN
EXPERIENCE . INTEGRITY . EXCELLENCE

agent inc.
REAL ESTATE
ELEVATED

MCMONIGLE
TEAM

REAL ESTATE'S BEST ADDRESS

DANIEL JI
REAL ESTATE IN STYLE

Physical Health Assessment ♥

0-1 doesn't match 2-3 partial match 4-5 strong match x put check mark in the related box

I do my best to avoid junk food.

| 0 | 1 | 2 | 3 | 4 | 5 |

If I can't devote time to a full workout, I still find something active to do on a daily basis.

| 0 | 1 | 2 | 3 | 4 | 5 |

Love Aspects To Focus On ♥   Recommended Reading ♥
Physical Health   The TB12 Method

Daily Schedule, Day 11.

AM	PM
06.00 His Word, First Word, Prayer	12.00
07.00 Exercise	01.00
08.00 Research Taglines You Like	02.00
09.00	03.00
10.00	04.00 Reach Out to Colleagues for Insight on a Few of Your Choices
11.00 Begin Writing a Tagline	05.00
	06.00 Home with Family
	07.00
	08.00 His Word, Last Word, Prayer

CREATE A LOGO

For no one does anything in secret when he himself seeks to be known publicly. If you do these things, show yourself to the world. (NASB)

John 7:4

Let's take a moment to think back to day 2, when you were learning how to visualize your future. The ability to envision tangible future experiences is a major step forward when it comes to finding your path, syncing up with God's plan, and bringing your goals to fruition. But visualization is also a key component when it comes to your clients. It's basic human nature to interpret and make decisions about products, homes, and people with our eyes first. This is called a first impression. So it's fair to say that your image and the first impression you make are important when it comes to building your business.

That said, many of your initial connections with clients won't come about through personal interactions—which means your brand image is the most important tool you have right now to engage a client and showcase your professionalism and dedication to servitude. But how do you grab someone's attention and make a good first impression without interacting with them immediately? Easy. Start with an eye-catching professional logo.

With Agentinc., you have access to a highly gifted graphic design team that is responsible for creating and generating the look and feel of our brand and your business across all platforms, ensuring that you receive the elevated level of visual representation an agent in your position deserves.

But not everyone possesses the gift of artistic vision. So how do you find a logo that not only fits your personality and expertise in real estate but also is on-brand with your brokerage? Here are a few pointers to get your graphic design imagination moving:

1. Research other agent designs.
2. Explore logos of brands that are in line with the consumer base you'd like to target.
3. Select a color scheme. To find the right color scheme for your business, look at what certain colors mean and what emotions they invoke.
   - Red—passion, love
   - Green—fertility, wealth, healing
   - Yellow—joy, intellect
   - Black—luxury, secrecy
   - White—perfection, purity, cleanliness
   - Blue—knowledge, trustworthiness, calm
   - Purple—royalty, wisdom, imagination
   - Orange—creativity, uniqueness, energy
   - Gray—sophisticated neutrality
4. Select fonts you like.
5. Know the "feel" of your logo.
   - Exotic
   - Sporty
   - Masculine
   - Feminine
   - Playful
   - Colorful
   - Modern

6. Select three points you'd like to communicate through your logo.
7. Imagine seeing your logo on the front of a hotel. What kind of hotel is it? Do people want to stay there?
8. Ask yourself, If this logo was on the corner of an NBA basketball jersey, would I notice it?

Once you have an idea of what you're looking for, reach out to Agentinc.'s team of design experts or choose a reliable site like logotournament.com to enhance your visual brand recognition.

PARADYME

Physical Health Assessment ♥

0-1 doesn't match   2-3 partial match   4-5 strong match   x put check mark in the related box

I make an effort each day to better my body.

`0` `1` `2` `3` `4` `5`

Each day I understand that my health is important to those who love me.

`0` `1` `2` `3` `4` `5`

Love Aspects To Focus On ♥   Recommended Reading ♥
Physical Health   The TB12 Method

Daily Schedule, Day 12. 🕐

AM	PM
06.00 His Word, First Word, Prayer	12.00
07.00 Exercise	01.00
08.00 Research Your Logo	02.00
09.00	03.00
10.00	04.00
11.00 Reach Out to the Agent Inc. Media Team or Choose a Logo Website	05.00
	06.00 Home with Family
	07.00
	08.00 His Word, Last Word, Prayer

START BUILDING YOUR CORE SUPPORT TEAM

Two are better than one, because they have a good return for their labor: If either of them falls down, one can help the other up. But pity anyone who falls and has no one to help them up. (NIV)

Ecclesiastes 4:9–10

J ust as the verse from Ecclesiastes states, "Two are better than one." Your success as a real estate agent depends not only on your dedication to servitude and excellence at your craft but also on your ability to find a team of people who will help you expand your brand while simultaneously providing professional and essential services to your clients. Now is the time to begin putting together a list of contractors and handymen, mortgage brokers, transaction coordinators (TCs), escrow officers, and title representatives.

Establishing solid relationships with your core team will help you streamline your schedule while simultaneously providing your clients with a stress-free transactional process. It's easy to think that once you have a buyer, a seller, or an offer, you have succeeded in what you set out to do. But it is vital to understand that just because there is an agreement in place doesn't mean your job is done. There are many failure points along the road to a success-ful transaction that can easily be avoided. By surrounding yourself with a trustworthy team of professionals, you can eliminate pitfalls and guarantee your chances of fulfillment.

But it's not just the paperwork and logistical assistance that your core support team helps you with—they can also be a vital component of your marketing campaign. Simply put: Your mort-gage broker wants you to succeed. Your escrow officer wants you to succeed. Your TC wants you to succeed. All of these people depend on your ability to close deals and are willing to do whatever they can to ensure that you are able to bring them business. Ask your mortgage broker to help subsidize mail costs and provide you with affordability flyers for your next open house. Select an escrow offi-cer who can help you and your clients quickly manage and close deals without stress, and ask them to provide estimated net sheets for deals you are working on. Find a TC you enjoy working with and can trust to ensure that each document is correct and com-plete, allowing you to focus on the core element of your job as an agent—servicing your clients and generating more listings.

Aside from establishing these valuable alliances, you should familiarize yourself with and forge a strong relationship with another important team member, your title representative. Today's title representatives wear many hats when it comes to helping agents. First and foremost, title reps are a rich resource for real estate marketing information and know-how, and have access to advanced technology and information designed to increase your client base and help you gain listings. But why should a title rep be such a big part of expanding your brand? Remember, the rela-tionship between agent and title representative is symbiotic. Yes, title representatives sell title insurance. But in order to sell title insurance, they must have a pipeline to agents who can bring them business. This is why title representatives are an essential ally when it comes to generating leads. Simply put, their success depends on your success.

By familiarizing yourself with and focusing on the
properties in your smart farm that may soon go to
market, you will be able to create a targeted strategy
that allows you to effectively spend your time on leads
that have a greater chance of coming to fruition.

As iron sharpens iron, so one person sharpens another. (NIV)
Proverbs 27:17

Now that you understand the importance of your title representative, let's discuss the smart farm. The smart farm is one of the most valuable assets your title representative can share with you. A smart farm provides analytics representing the percentage of homes most likely to sell in the next one to two years. As we have touched upon and will discuss later, time management is crucial to brand expansion, mental health, and financial success in real estate. Your primary function as an agent should be increasing your visibility through marketing, connecting with and networking with potential clients, and generating listings. To properly fulfill these responsibilities takes time and dedication. In order to dedicate the time required to expand, you must first find a way to streamline your business. By familiarizing yourself with and focusing on the properties in your smart farm that may soon go to market, you will be able to create a targeted strategy that allows you to effectively spend your time on leads that have a greater chance of coming to fruition.

When seeking out a relationship with a title representative, it's important to do your research. Ask agents you admire who they feel is an integral part of their team and system, and ask for an introduction. When selecting a title rep, it's important to choose someone you feel you will be able to maintain a personal and professional relationship with over a long period of time. They should be experts on your farm and understand marketing trends as well as your competition.

As an Agentinc. agent, once you've begun developing your team you can use the Agentinc. software to promote your team members on your Agentinc. neighborhood website. By surrounding yourself with the finest, most knowledgeable, and most determined teammates, you are creating a formula for success.

Teamwork is not a preference, it is a requirement.

John Wooden

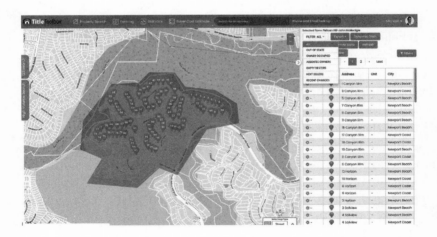

Physical Health Assessment ♥

0-1 doesn't match   2-3 partial match   4-5 strong match   x put check mark in the related box

I enjoy physical activity.

`0`☐ `1`☐ `2`☐ `3`☐ `4`☐ `5`☐

I feel a sense of accomplishment when I finish a workout.

`0`☐ `1`☐ `2`☐ `3`☐ `4`☐ `5`☐

Love Aspects To Focus On ♥
Physical Health

Recommended Reading ♥
The TB12 Method

Daily Schedule, Day 13. 🕐

AM

06.00 His Word, First Word, Prayer

07.00 Exercise

08.00 Research Your Core Support Team

09.00

10.00

11.00

PM

12.00

01.00 Reach Out to Your Top Choices for Support Team

02.00

03.00

04.00

05.00

06.00 Home with Family

07.00

08.00 His Word, Last Word, Prayer

STUDY YOUR FARM

Do not forsake wisdom, and she will protect you; love her, and she will watch over you. The beginning of wisdom is this: Get wisdom. Though it cost all you have, get understanding. (NIV)

Proverbs 4:6–7

Specialist—a person who concentrates primarily on a particular subject or activity; a person highly skilled in a specific and restricted field.

Gaining wisdom and becoming a "specialist" in any field requires an immense amount of discipline and devotion to your subject. But God has given you the tools you need to "get wisdom," to become a "specialist." It isn't enough to simply familiarize yourself with information pertinent to your industry—you must work to differentiate yourself, to obtain a perspective unlike anyone else before you.

In order to become an expert in the real estate industry, it is imperative that you become truly devoted to attaining all the relevant information and knowledge about your farm and client base, allowing you to not only stand out as the preeminent source for service and expertise, but also to gain trust and loyalty among your peers, your teammates, and your farm.

When I began tending my Lido Isle, Newport Beach, farm several years ago, I made an agreement with myself and with God to become the most knowledgeable and dedicated agent in my area. And by using the talents and intellect God gave me, I was able to "get understanding," to achieve my goal and differentiate myself from my fellow agents.

But how does an agent go about becoming a specialist in their farm? First, I bought a three-ring binder. In this three-ring binder, I created tabs for every street in my farm. Under each tab, I wrote down every address. Each day, I researched the addresses. Who owned the houses? When did they last sell? How much did they sell for? Who lives there currently? Do they have a pet? What kind of car do they drive? What are their children's names?

I added to my binder every piece of information I was able to glean from the internet, multiple listing service (MLS), and conversations with friends, acquaintances, strangers, and neighbors. As I continued to accumulate information, I studied it. When I would meet someone at a coffee shop and hand them my card, I'd ask where they lived. And when they replied with the street, I would be able to mentally recall it and exhibit my wisdom and expertise. My ability to stimulate a conversation about a specific neighborhood would leave a lasting impression. My ability to recollect people, parks, restaurants, schools, salons, tailors, and even specific homes I loved on that particular street would build my client's confidence in my expertise.

"My ability to stimulate a conversation about a specific neighborhood would leave a lasting impression."

My three-ring binder gave me insight into and access to everyone in my farm. At open houses, I would ask visitors where they lived and what their names were. If I couldn't immediately recall something specific about their home, I would look it up in the binder, circle back to them, and immediately find a way into a conversation that showcased my expertise, my knowledge, my understanding, and my dedication to my farm.

Becoming a successful real estate agent requires the motivation to use the talents and intellect God has given you to their maximum capabilities. To be truly great at any occupation, from brain surgeon to plumber to agent, requires a promise and commitment to become as knowledgeable and skilled as possible, as well as to provide the level of servitude and grace God expects from you.

Take time each day to add something to the binder you now possess. Study your farm. Get wisdom. Get understanding. By differentiating yourself as a neighborhood specialist and expert devoted to the nuances and beauty of your farm, you are creating an important and strong bond with those you service.

To present yourself as a neighborhood specialist, you should know the following things:

1. Year your farm was developed
2. Developer of your farm
3. Company that graded the lots
4. Utility companies involved in the development
5. Year the utilities went underground
6. Civil engineers who built nearby developments
7. Price that the original lots or houses sold for
8. Annual appreciation to date
9. Demographics
10. Median household income
11. Unemployment rate
12. Neighborhood amenities, such as guard gate, clubhouse, playground, tennis courts, golf course, waterfront, guest docks, walkways, retail plaza, pool, and volleyball courts

13. Nearby private and public schools
14. Churches
15. Air quality
16. Crime rating
17. Earthquake frequency and intensity
18. Number and names of subdivisions
19. All current utility companies branded for distribution
20. Average age of property
21. Current cost to build
22. Members of the design review board and review criteria
23. Homeowners Association (HOA) and dues
24. CC&Rs
25. Prominent vendors, builders, and architects
26. Indigenous plants
27. General soils report
28. Title 24 (California Energy Code)
29. Property tax rate
30. Assessments, if any
31. Litigation
32. Average days of sunshine
33. Industry
34. Job growth
35. Current market trends
36. Average age
37. Local charities
38. Cultural rituals and holidays
39. Local hotels
40. City manager, governor, and mayor
41. Trash day
42. Parking ordinances
43. Pet ordinances
44. Local fire department
45. Local police chief

46. Local hospitals
47. Vendors
48. Most common reason people move to your farm
49. Most common reason people move away from your farm
50. Local sports teams
51. Record sale
52. Best deal right now
53. Current style trends

Physical Health Assessment ♥
0-1 doesn't match   2-3 partial match   4-5 strong match   x put check mark in the related box

I make a conscious effort to eat foods that will make me feel good.

| 0 | | 1 | | 2 | | 3 | | 4 | | 5 | |

I feel the need to continue taking care of my body on a daily basis.

| 0 | | 1 | | 2 | | 3 | | 4 | | 5 | |

Love Aspects To Focus On ♥   Recommended Reading ♥
Physical Health   The TB12 Method

Daily Schedule, Day 14.

AM

06.00 His Word, First Word, Prayer

07.00 Exercise

08.00 Study Your Farm

09.00 Add Farm Information to
      Your Binder

10.00

11.00

PM

12.00

01.00

02.00

03.00

04.00

05.00

06.00 Home with Family

07.00

08.00 His Word, Last Word, Prayer

Know also that wisdom is like honey for you: If you find it, there is a future hope for you, and your hope will not be cut off. (NIV)

Proverbs 24:14

Days
15-28

BLUEPRINT FOR SUCCESS

O Lord, You are my God; I will exalt You, I will give thanks to Your name; For You have worked wonders, plans formed long ago, with perfect faithfulness. (NASB)

Isaiah 25:1

The palace at Versailles. The Taj Mahal. St. Basil's Cathedral. The ancient city of Jerusalem. These masterpieces of architecture weren't built in a day. They took careful planning, a dedication to craft, and a realistic vision. God has a plan for you, and it's quite simple—seek and surrender to His divine will and give Him thanks for all He does for you, and He will continue to expertly guide you with His partnership.

When you set out to achieve your goal—be it building a cathedral or establishing a career as a real estate agent—it is important to create a blueprint that can serve as a guide to help you realize your vision.

Included in the Recommended Reading section on page xi is a book titled *Blueprint for Success*, written by my ex-father-in-law, Joe Weller, CEO of Nestlé USA. Throughout our relationship, Joe influenced my career in a number of positive ways. Over the years, I've developed the utmost respect for Joe's ability to dissect business and take action. His book can be interpreted as a proud and cultural perspective based on the ideology of "If it is meant to be, it is up to me." Although this notion is somewhat contrary to the Christian belief that God created us with a plan in mind, I choose to interpret his message in another way. The best-selling author and founder of Saddleback Church, Pastor Rick Warren, explains that God has given us a brain, freedom of choice, and an abundance of talents and that He constructed us and wired us to build and create in His image. That said, our blueprint is subject to God's will. We will be successful, as we like to say back in Oklahoma, "Lord willing and the creek don't rise"—which essentially means we must give God all the glory, surrender our will to His divine plan, and ask for His guidance and blessing while using our spiritual motivation to take the balance of matters into our own hands. The heart of the matter is a matter of the heart.

Below you'll see Agentinc.'s Blueprint for Success, as well as your own streamlined Blueprint for Success. I believe it is a great exercise, and I encourage you to personalize it, keep it close, and revisit it often.

AGENTINC. BLUEPRINT FOR SUCCESS

Agentinc. offers a robust multichannel platform built by agents, for agents, to ensure that our associates have the tools needed to develop a successful career. Our Blueprint for Success is founded upon four core elements:

Vision: What Agentinc. Strives to Be

We define the future. In order to become the best real estate firm in the country, we commit ourselves wholly to our vision. We possess the discipline and determination to bring our ideals to fruition. Agentinc. is dedicated to becoming the best it is capable of being. We own and understand the Agentinc. brand.

Strategies: How We Intend to Get There

Innovation: What steps can we take to reach our goal? We consistently revitalize our brand and always maintain a high level of awareness when it comes to new technology as well as advertising and media platforms. We are committed to expanding our digital marketing and AI capabilities.

Experience: We are dedicated to maintaining a high level of service across all aspects of real estate, from mortgages to home inspections to vendor services. Our continued commitment to evolving with industry trends generates respect and loyalty from our clients.

Communication: Agentinc. continues to build relationships with agents, vendors, and clients across the globe. We are open to critique and constructive criticism and will utilize this information to expand and improve.

Efficiency: We are always seeking new technological and social avenues to streamline our agent and client experiences.

Measures: How We Know When We Are There

Vision: We redefine our vision each year and are dedicated to improving our service, expanding our brand, and creating improved fiscal futures for our team.

Growth: We aim to achieve a 10 percent increase in revenue each year.

Core Values: Our Belief System

People: We exhibit our core values to associates and clients each and every day. We are dedicated to leadership, service, and stewardship.

Brand: We are consistent with brand messaging and are dedicated to expanding the brand across all media platforms.

Clients: Our dedication to service is what sets us apart in real estate. We are committed to assisting all our clients not only with their real estate endeavors but also with their personal futures.

Full Service: Agentinc. aims to create a streamlined process for its agents and clients across all spectrums of the real estate industry. We encourage our agents and clients to work directly with our ancillary companies to provide a holistically efficient and rewarding real estate experience.

Performance: We use our core values to achieve the highest level of success.

Commit to the Lord whatever you do, and he will establish your plans. (NIV)

Proverbs 16:3

Your Blueprint for Success

Create 3/6/12-month goals based on these same four core elements. Maintaining a 3/6/12-month goal schedule based on your vision, strategies, measures, and core values will allow you to consistently be aware of what your focus, time, and energy should be, and is being, used on. These goals should be well-rounded and based on not only financial and career growth but also spiritual and physical growth. Your ability to increase revenue, sell homes, and manage your time is directly related to your growth as a human. When we find ourselves acting with a Christian purpose at the forefront of our actions, we generate love and hope. When we generate love and hope, we open our hearts and souls to opportunities—we become magnetic. Creating goals with faith, hope, and love will not only fulfill your vocational responsibilities but also fulfill your responsibilities to your clients, yourself, and your loved ones.

"Creating goals with faith, hope, and love will not only
fulfill your vocational responsibilities but also fulfill your
responsibilities to your clients, yourself, and your loved ones."

Now, it may be difficult to set forth realistic goals for each of
these milestones—everyone wants to sell 15 homes in their first
three months. So, when setting your goals, it's important to realize
where you are on your journey as an agent and to set goals that
are achievable and valuable. Yes, your goals as an agent should be
to increase your client base, offer the best service, collect listings,
and generate income. But to accomplish these goals, you must meet
several smaller goals first.

Try to look at your career as if you were building a pyramid.
The foundation of being a successful real estate agent is your ability
to create a wealth of knowledge about your farm and to create a
CRM that allows you to share this knowledge with your clients. At
Agentinc. we've created proprietary software that can evaluate and
compute your probability of success as an agent through our intu-
itive Elevated CRM, which tracks the average sale price in your
farm, your dedication to outreach, and your commitment to holding open houses, as well as several other factors we discuss in this
book. By tracking your daily routine and commitment to growing
as an agent, you can see exactly what you can expect in return for
your hard work and stewardship.

BLUEPRINT FOR SUCCESS

Create 3/6/12-Month Goals Based on These Four Elements:

Vision: Who You Want to Be

Define your future. In order to become a successful agent, you must wholly commit yourself to your vision of the future. You must create a plan, practice patience, and possess the discipline and determination to bring your ideals to fruition. You must become the best you are capable of being. To start, ask yourself this question: Who do I want to be, and how do I want to feel? Own and understand your brand. Make sure you are exactly who you want to be on paper, in personal interactions, and online. Understand that your mind can lead you directly to where you want to be. You have the road map right here in front of you—simply take the first step.

Strategies: How You Intend to Get There

Innovation: What steps will you take to reach your goal? Consistently revitalize your brand, and always maintain a high level of awareness when it comes to new technology as well as advertising and media platforms.

Experience: Dedicate yourself to gaining experience in all aspects of real estate, from mortgages to home inspections to pool care. Keep learning to keep earning. By becoming an expert in your field, you will gain the respect and loyalty of your clients.

Communication: Build relationships with fellow agents, vendors, and your core support team. Find a mentor you can learn from, and expand your network. Always ask respected associates and acquaintances for feedback. Know that critiques and constructive criticism will help you realize your vision.

Efficiency: Manage your time and focus on accomplishing your 3/6/12-month goals.

Measures: How You Know When You Are There

Vision: How will you know when you have achieved your vision? What definitive and tangible goals can you set for yourself? Declare these goals to yourself and to others, and work backward through your vision of success to identify the steps necessary to achieve your ultimate goals.

Growth: Aim to achieve a 10 percent increase in revenue each year.

Core Values: Your Belief System

People: Exhibit your core values to your associates and clients each and every day. Develop an executive presence and become a leader and specialist in your farm. Most importantly, lead by example.

Brand: Remain consistent with messaging and continue to expand your brand.

Clients: Your dedication to service is what sets you apart in your field. Make a commitment to assist the residents in your farm not only with their real estate endeavors but also with their personal futures.

Full Service: Create a streamlined process for your clients by working directly with Agentinc.'s ancillary companies built for all agents. This will allow you to provide a holistically efficient and beneficial real estate experience.

Performance: Use your core values to achieve the highest level of success.

> "For I know the plans I have for you," declares the Lord, "plans to prosper you and not to harm you, plans to give you hope and a future." (NIV)
>
> **Jeremiah 29:11**

Have a look at a few goals you can set for yourself today that will maximize your probability of success over the next 12 months:

- Add vendors to your neighborhood specialist page.
- Fill in the pages of your three-ring binder within six months.
- Establish how many open houses you intend to hold over the next 3/6/12 months.
- Set your Revenue Share recruitment goals.
- Establish how many auction properties you will represent.
- Purchase an investment in your farm. At some point, you need to stop working for money and let your money work for you.

By setting a defined list of goals and meeting them every 3/6/12 months, you can feel confident that you are not only growing as an agent but also furthering your career and developing your expertise by dedicating yourself to a routine of successfully completing what you set out to accomplish.

Mental Health Assessment ✎

0-1 doesn't match 2-3 partial match 4-5 strong match x put check mark in the related box

I feel good about myself and my career.

0️⃣ 1️⃣ 2️⃣ 3️⃣ 4️⃣ 5️⃣

When I look in the mirror, I see someone who is happy.

0️⃣ 1️⃣ 2️⃣ 3️⃣ 4️⃣ 5️⃣

I accept others and use my faith to bring happiness to those around me.

0️⃣ 1️⃣ 2️⃣ 3️⃣ 4️⃣ 5️⃣

Love Aspects To Focus On ✎
Mental Health

Recommended Reading ✎
A Blueprint for Success

Daily Schedule, Day 15. 🕐

AM		PM	
06.00	His Word, First Word, Prayer	12.00	
07.00	Exercise	01.00	
08.00	Establish Your 3, 6, 12 Month Goals	02.00	
09.00		03.00	
10.00		04.00	
11.00	Take Steps to Increase Your Probability of Success	05.00	
		06.00	Home with Family
		07.00	
		08.00	His Word, Last Word, Prayer

SET UP SOCIAL MEDIA ACCOUNTS FOR YOUR BUSINESS

But he said to them, "I must preach the good news of the kingdom of God to the other towns as well; for I was sent for this purpose." (ESV)

Luke 4:43

By devoting ourselves to our community, whether through our church or our neighborhood, we enable ourselves to connect with others on a personal level. A collective conscious is a set of shared beliefs, ideas, and moral attitudes that operate as a unifying force within society. When we reach out to our community in acts of servitude, we are furthering our success as a society and spreading the Good News. Today, social media is a major aspect of our socialization. Most people spend over two hours a day networking on social media. Because we have such powerful tools to connect with people in ways never imagined before, it is important to effectively utilize them to build your network, increase farm presence, and offer service and enlightenment to those who are looking for your guidance.

Many agents think that simply posting an open house on Instagram is enough to generate traffic and attract buyers. This is not the case. Because Instagram and Facebook have changed their algorithms to increase social activity among real users and decrease the impact of "influencers" on their followers, it is now more important than ever to be vigilant, consistent, and exact when it comes to posting your real estate listings and events on social media.

But the hows, whens, whys, and wheres of social media posting are subjects that many of us never had the chance to study in school. So, in order to get yourself started and begin successfully branding your business across social media, it's important to follow these specific steps:

1. **Set up your social media accounts.**
   This can be a time-consuming process but will be worthwhile in the long run. Ensure that your profile is set up as a business account, and allow people to contact you via your business page rather than your personal account. Once you have successfully set up your professional account, add your DRE license number and brokerage tag (@agentinc. co) to your bio.

"Your clients and potential clients want
to see who their agent really is."

---

2. **Follow your neighborhood farm.**
   To find your neighborhood farm on Instagram, click the search icon and enter "#yourfarm." Once you've found your farm, simply click "follow." Be sure to comment on the photos and stories being posted, and engage with users and followers daily.

3. **Post content that is 60 percent real estate, 40 percent lifestyle.**

   When people follow you on social media, they're more interested in who you are and what you do as a person than in what you're trying to sell. Your clients and potential clients want to see who their agent really is. Because of this, it's important to remain authentic yet respectful. Keep personal ideology and beliefs at bay, remain authentic and true to yourself, and share the fun and success of your real estate career and personal life in an engaging and respectful way. Remember, no one wants to work with a real estate robot—they want someone who experiences the same things they do, right there in the same neighborhood.

4. **Stick to a weekly routine.**

   A weekly routine is key to successful social media marketing. Create a social media calendar with scheduled pictures, comments, and hashtags for each week, and post them accordingly. By consistently posting, you have a better chance of being seen and followed.

5. **Hold contests within your farm area.**

   Everyone loves winning contests! Partner with a local business and offer a gift from that business as a prize. To increase visibility for your contest, tag people in your farm area who may be potential clients and send them supplemental postcards telling them to keep an eye on your social media accounts in order to win. The simple gesture of giving goes a long way when it comes to building a reputation in service. Plus, by partnering with local businesses, you can build up your referral network while providing them with their own free marketing—that's a win-win for everyone.

6. **Convey a consistent message and theme.**

   When it comes to a professional social media account, a consistent message directly reflects your organizational and branding skills. Take a look at a few successful brand accounts. What do you notice about their style, tone, and voice? Do you see any similarities? By keeping your messaging, filters, subjects, and voice consistent, you inherently speak to a certain level of professionalism, while also clearly displaying your commitment as an agent and your ability to communicate to potential buyers on behalf of your clients. Also, if possible, try to keep the same aesthetic and color scheme across the entire account—our eyes are drawn to organized and beautiful visual displays.

And remember, if you have any trouble at all creating or expanding your social media pages, you can reach out to our marketing department for tips that will help add followers and expand your reach.

Mental Health Assessment ✎

0-1 doesn't match   2-3 partial match   4-5 strong match   x put check mark in the related box

I understand my purpose in life.

`0` `1` `2` `3` `4` `5`

Each day, I strive for personal growth.

`0` `1` `2` `3` `4` `5`

I am open to new ideas, opportunities, and insights that can help me both spiritually and professionally.

`0` `1` `2` `3` `4` `5`

Love Aspects To Focus On ✎   Recommended Reading ✎
Relational Health   A Blueprint for Success

Daily Schedule, Day 16. 🕐

AM		PM	
06.00	His Word, First Word, Prayer	12.00	Networking Lunch
07.00	Exercise	01.00	Create Social Media Content
08.00	Set Up Social Media Accounts	02.00	
09.00		03.00	
10.00	Familiarize Yourself with Accounts in Your Farm	04.00	
11.00	Accumulate Followers in Your Farm	05.00	
		06.00	Home with Family
		07.00	
		08.00	His Word, Last Word, Prayer

FIND AND SCHEDULE YOUR FIRST OPEN HOUSE

Do not neglect to show hospitality to strangers, for by this some have entertained angels without knowing it. (NASB)

Hebrews 13:2

An agent's perceived value boils down to "How many qualified people can they turn out to an event?" How would you sell someone the fact that you are the "specialist" that is most influential and capable of results?

I cannot stress the importance of dedicating yourself to learning how to effectively operate and create a successful open house. Simply put, agents who have the discipline to hold open houses frequently and who make an effort to hold one every weekend have a 90 percent chance of becoming successful in their careers. Having built several successful brokerage companies and hired hundreds of agents over the years, I can say unequivocally that a vast majority of the agents who occupy the top 10 percent in sales are in the habit of holding open houses in the same neighborhood every single weekend.

The open house was the cornerstone of my career in real estate. Every weekend, I made it a point to have a sign in the ground somewhere in my farm. I made it a point to show up early and make the proper adjustments to the house, be it vacuuming, doing a bit of cleaning, opening windows, airing out the property, or fluffing pillows—whatever needed to be done to present the home in the best manner possible. I scheduled my open houses over the course of several hours during the weekend, giving everyone a chance to see the property regardless of their engagements. I arrived early and I left late. Neighbors and potential clients would see my car parked in front of that house hour after hour as a testament to my work ethic, my tenacity, my expertise, and my dedication to the neighborhood.

But there are challenges when it comes to scheduling open houses. You may be a new agent without a property to represent, and thus with no open house to showcase your talent and exhibit your tenacity, work ethic, expertise, and dedication. But that shouldn't stop you. To successfully hold an open house, you need practice. It was one month before I held an open house and six months before I landed my first listing. You may be asking yourself, How did John hold an open house if he didn't have his own listing?

Here are a couple of tips to get the ball rolling:

1. **Ask another agent.**
   Connect with an agent who represents multiple properties, and ask if you can hold their open house with no strings attached. Explain that whether or not you represent a buyer, you'll send potential clients directly to them. More likely than not, that agent will gratefully accept your help, allowing them to manage their own time effectively while you do a little legwork.

―――――――――

"Once you have secured your first open house, it's
important to arrive early and drive and walk the
neighborhood, introducing yourself to those in your
farm who may be looking for an agent themselves."

―――――――――

2. **Reach out to developers in your farm.**
    If you don't have an agent in mind who can help, try reaching out to builders and managers of new developments in your farm. Ask if they mind if you set up shop outside their new construction and discuss salient information on the upcoming properties with interested people. By doing this seemingly "free work," you have actually found a way to consistently create a presence in your farm and build a relationship with the builders in your community.

Once you have secured your first open house, it's important to arrive early and drive and walk the neighborhood, introducing yourself to those in your farm who may be looking for an agent themselves. It takes tenacity to land your first listing—and that should be your main goal. Remember, chasing buyers is a time-consuming process that can detract from your progress and cause you to lose focus from your goal of accruing listings. By focusing exclusively on finding listings and holding open houses, you can begin building your neighborhood presence—and then the buyers will come to you.

Mental Health Assessment ✂
0-1 doesn't match   2-3 partial match   4-5 strong match   x put check mark in the related box

I make my own decisions based on the teachings of Christ.

[0] [1] [2] [3] [4] [5]

I shape my environment whenever possible and adjust to it when necessary.

[0] [1] [2] [3] [4] [5]

I am independent and autonomous in my thinking and in my career.

[0] [1] [2] [3] [4] [5]

Love Aspects To Focus On ✂   Recommended Reading ✂
Mental Health   A Blueprint for Success

Daily Schedule, Day 17. 🕐

AM	PM
06.00 His Word, First Word, Prayer	12.00
07.00 Exercise	01.00
08.00 Dedicate Yourself to Acquiring Your First Open House	02.00
09.00	03.00
10.00	04.00
11.00	05.00
	06.00 Home with Family
	07.00
	08.00 His Word, Last Word, Prayer

CREATE YOUR NETWORK OF VENDORS AND MERCHANTS WITH THE COMMUNITY ELEVATED PROGRAM

And do not forget to do good and to share with others, for with such sacrifices God is pleased. (NIV)

Hebrews 13:16

When we act with others in mind, helping everyone around us to succeed, we create success both spiritually and financially for ourselves. When you support local businesses, local brokers, local vendors, and local merchants by generating referrals and business for them, you are creating an environment and relationship based upon love and hope. When people experience random kindness, it fills them with love and gratitude. By being selfless, you are representing yourself as a leader in the community and someone who is dedicated to the success of their farm—not just themselves.

As you know, Agentinc.'s business model is unique because it encourages agents to become neighborhood specialists through the Buy a Neighborhood Program. By claiming a specific neighborhood in your farm, you can market yourself as an "expert" in your geographic region, building confidence not only for residents within your neighborhood and farm but also for the vendors and merchants who provide essential home services within that area.

> Do nothing out of selfish ambition or vain conceit. Rather, in humility value others above yourselves, not looking to your own interests but each of you to the interests of the others. (NIV)
> **Philippians 2:3–4**

Networking is a powerful tool that should be utilized in all aspects of our lives. When God made man and woman, he envisioned a community. Your willingness to become involved in your farm—to invest your time, your service, and your charity in your community—allows you to distinguish yourself as someone who truly believes in the people you are surrounded by.

In our line of work, we have a seemingly infinite number of opportunities to help our communities. When we are able to recommend a pool cleaner or an architect or an interior designer or an electrician, we are helping our community become more successful. These selfless acts rarely go unnoticed. Think of the last time someone referred your services, your talents, or your wisdom to a stranger. How did that make you feel? If you're anything like me, you felt blessed, thankful, and filled with hope and happiness. When we surround ourselves with these emotions and we commit ourselves to not only those who can help us attain our career goals but also those who will benefit from our success, we are truly living in a balanced, symbiotic relationship with both humanity and God. God wants us all to thrive. When we act with servitude and loyalty in mind, we create a two-way street of kindness and generosity that consistently benefits both parties, injecting financial and spiritual prosperity into our community.

With the Agentinc. Vendor Program, you can provide vendors with the unique ability to establish a profitable network and gain optimal visibility through a multitude of advertising, publication, web, and social media platforms. By offering your vendors the opportunity to work directly with the Agentinc. marketing and sales teams to promote their services, you ensure that your partners reach a vast range of prospective clients who are looking for established providers backed by the Agentinc. name. By joining the Vendor Program, vendors gain access to Agentinc.'s innovative marketing and advertising strategies, giving them the ability to expand their reach in their desired neighborhood or region at a fraction of the cost of other advertising channels. It's also important to note that both the Buy a Neighborhood Program and the Vendor Program are designed to not only help agents offset the costs of their neighborhood purchase but also generate passive income. For each vendor added to the Vendor Program, agents receive 25 percent of the setup fee and 25 percent of the vendor's recurring monthly subscription.

If you've decided to become an Agentinc. agent, you should research our Buy a Neighborhood Program today. After the Agentinc. sales and marketing team begins adding vendors to your neighborhood, make sure you familiarize yourself with the people, businesses, and vendors that you will be interacting with when clients begin or continue to ask you for recommendations. Reach out to these friends, businesses, and vendors and introduce yourself. Explain to them that you are excited to work with them and will refer business whenever the opportunity arises. Explain that if they or anyone they know would like assistance in their real estate endeavors, you would love to meet with them.

When we open ourselves up to our community by providing service and stimulating the micro-economy within it, we are opening ourselves up to opportunity. We are displaying a willingness to help those within our geographic sphere, and we are exemplifying what it means to live with the interests of others at the forefront of our motivation.

To begin building your network of vendors and merchants, purchase a neighborhood through our Buy a Neighborhood Program and give yourself the opportunity to not only bring in referrals but also generate passive income. By familiarizing yourself with the people who define your community, you will place yourself in a position to bring people together while becoming a central and integral part of your neighborhood's identity.

"The Agentinc. Smart Booth is a powerful tool that should be placed at well-visited landmarks in your area, including car washes, airports, grocery stores, automotive service centers, hospital waiting rooms, and theaters."

Also, now is the time to contact our marketing department to receive your Smart Booth. The Agentinc. Smart Booth is a powerful tool that should be placed at well-visited landmarks in your area, including car washes, airports, grocery stores, automotive service centers, hospital waiting rooms, and theaters. The Smart Booth allows potential clients to explore your neighborhood while funneling their information directly to your CRM, allowing you to effortlessly generate leads that can build your brand.

Agentinc. Rewards Program

The Agentinc. Rewards Program is designed to incentivize and nurture business and professional relationships among agents, neighborhood vendors, and clients. By participating in the Agentinc. Rewards Program, agents, vendors, and clients can gain cash rewards on their Elevated Rewards card each time they refer a service, place an ad in *Elevated* magazine, or use one of the 20 ancillary Agentinc. companies.

How It Works for Agents

When an Agentinc. agent purchases a neighborhood through the Buy a Neighborhood Program, our sales team immediately approaches local vendors about being promoted on the agent's neighborhood website. Once vendors agree to the terms of the

Vendor Program, the Agentinc. media department begins using a multichannel marketing strategy to enhance visibility and promote the vendor's business. Clients located within the neighborhood are given a 15 percent discount on the services each vendor provides. An additional 15 percent referral fee goes directly to the agent for each successful completion of the services provided by the vendor—it's that simple.

The Agentinc. Rewards Program also applies to our Revenue Share Program. Whenever an agent you have recruited uses one of our vendors or ancillary companies, you earn cash rewards.

With the Agentinc. Rewards Program, agents can access their dashboard to check and maintain current balances as well as keep track of incoming cash rewards.

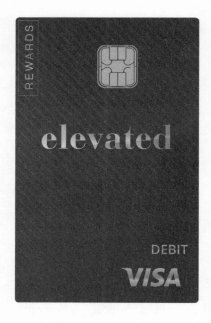

How It Works for Vendors

As part of the Agentinc. Vendor Program, vendors gain access to our innovative marketing team and enjoy optimal visibility on all of Agentinc.'s advertising, publication, web, and social media platforms. With the Rewards Program, vendors are asked to provide a small markdown for services in exchange for Agentinc.'s strategic marketing and advertising campaigns. Each time a vendor provides services for an Agentinc. agent, refers an Agentinc. agent to a client, or places an ad in *Elevated* magazine, they receive cash rewards that can be spent on anything anywhere in the world.

How It Works for Buyers and Sellers

The Agentinc. Rewards Program also gives back to each of our esteemed clients. When a buyer or seller uses any of Agentinc.'s companies to purchase or sell a home, they also receive cash rewards on their Elevated Rewards card. Agentinc. is built to provide all our agents and their clients with world-class service designed to streamline the transactional process while simultaneously incentivizing the use of our partners and vendors.

Mental Health Assessment ✌

0-1 doesn't match   2-3 partial match   4-5 strong match   x put check mark in the related box

I consistently find beauty in my daily life.

`0` `1` `2` `3` `4` `5`

I have positive relationships with my friends, family, and loved ones.

`0` `1` `2` `3` `4` `5`

I have a harmonious relationship between body and mind.

`0` `1` `2` `3` `4` `5`

I do not become overwhelmed by emotions such as fear, anger, love, jealousy, guilt, or anxiety.

`0` `1` `2` `3` `4` `5`

Love Aspects To Focus On ✌   Recommended Reading ✌
Mental Health   A Blueprint for Success

Daily Schedule, Day 18. 🕐

AM		PM	
06.00	His Word, First Word, Prayer	12.00	
07.00	Exercise	01.00	Buy a Neighborhood
08.00	Research the Buy a Neighborhood Program	02.00	
09.00		03.00	
10.00		04.00	
11.00	Familiarize Yourself with the Vendor Program	05.00	
		06.00	Home with Family
		07.00	
		08.00	His Word, Last Word, Prayer

LIST TO LAST: PREPARE YOUR ULTIMATE LISTING PRESENTATION

> You will make known to me the path of life; In Your presence is fullness of joy; In Your right hand there are pleasures forever. (NASB)
>
> **Psalm 16:11**

There's a saying you may have heard in our industry: "List to last." God has given us a path to follow, but it is our duty to stay on that path and receive eternal joy. I believe that in order to live a successful life in real estate both spiritually and financially, it's important to focus on the elements that will provide longevity and long-term sustainability for both your spirit and your finances.

Throughout my career, I've noticed that there are two different kinds of agents: listing agents and buyers' agents. I'll make this easy for you—those of you who are focused on becoming listing agents will have a long and profitable future. Those of you who are not, most likely won't. Right now, your listing goals should be simple—gain 12 listings in your farm. If you can secure 12 listings, you will turn over a property each month of the year. You will have 12 signs in the ground. You will have 12 contracts signed. And most important, you will have revenue you can count on. If you are focused on perpetually chasing buyers, believing they will eventually commit to a property, you are in fact wasting valuable time. As I mentioned before, once you have a listing, buyers will come to you. Remember, the people in your farm are watching you, and your ability to list in your farm is immensely valuable to your brand image in the long term. The residents of your farm see your signs, they see your marketing materials, they research your days on market, and most of all they see you—your car, your work ethic, your positive presence in their neighborhood. By listing in your farm and remaining dedicated to becoming a fixture within it, you will build trust and gain recognition, two immensely important factors when sellers select an agent.

But some of you may still be looking for your first listing or may not know how to reframe your career to place the utmost importance on securing listings. If you are in this position, it is time to order your Agentinc. listing presentation box or create one of your own. Once you receive or create your listing presentation box, immediately begin familiarizing yourself with every detail of your farm. Memorize each bullet point. Reach out to your marketing department for a professional copywriter who can help with your advertising and listings. If you're an Agentinc. agent, ask our marketing department to add your name to the front and back covers of *Elevated* magazine, Agentinc.'s in-house publication dedicated to luxury listings, local and international cuisine, design, building, and lifestyle. By placing your name in our professional publication, you will gain instant credibility as an agent, proving to your farm that you are a dedicated professional who can deliver elite results.

Your ability to win in the living room is the difference between a long and prosperous real estate career and a short-lived fling in the industry. In order to win in the living room, it is important to follow these steps to ensure success:

1. **Order or create your listing presentation box and begin adding information.**

2. **Order and prioritize your materials.**
   Go through your listing materials and structure your presentation in a way that is both compelling and natural.
3. **Secure and elevate your listing with a biweekly property report.**
   Agentinc.'s biweekly property report is a powerful, digital, and customized pre-listing tool that allows you to research exactly what your client is most interested in when it comes to fulfilling their real estate endeavors. By simply emailing our Agentinc. pre-listing property report to your prospective client, you can gain access to advantageous marketing analytics that will assist you in landing your listing, as well as meeting and exceeding your client's expectations. The biweekly report is also available post-listing and provides your client with all the information they need to stay informed during the selling process.

REPORTS

CALENDAR REPORT   click to view

Marketing, showings, action items

ONLINE MARKETING   click to view

Industry's most extensive online marketing program

COMPARABLE PROPERTIES   click to view

Competitive market analysis of your property

OC LUXURY REPORT   click to view

Current stats on the luxury market in Orange County

INTERNET MARKETING

GLOBAL MARKETING   click to view

Global marketing to over 100 trusted international websites

NATIONWIDE EXPOSURE   click to view

Industry's most extensive online marketing program

EMAIL FLYER   click to view

40K plus distribution through private database

PROPERTY LISTING   click to view

Agent version of your property in the MLS

PRINT MARKETING

BROCHURES   click to view

Distinctive brochure showcasing your home

4. **Become comfortable with communicating.**
   If you aren't a people person, now is the time to make a change. Your willingness to communicate will show potential clients that you are able to go the extra mile to secure their listings.

   Start by listening.
   We are often so anxious to impress we forget to listen.

   Use a little humor.
   I like to self-deprecate by saying, "Before I open this box of shameless self-promotion, let's talk about you, your goals, and your recent experiences with this asset."

   Then present your listings.
   Once you feel you have a good grasp and have established that you care, dig into your listing presentation.

5. **Hone your ability to market locally and globally.**
   Your ability to convey your expertise to your farm and the world at large is dependent on your marketing messaging and tone.

6. **Choose three sale prices.**
   Give your client an estimated shelf life at each price range, and give them the power to choose a price based on their timeline.

7. **Prepare the replacement analysis.**
   This helpful tool will allow your clients to more easily understand the value of their home when entering the market.

8. **Be responsive.**
   Your availability is important when it comes to satisfying client demands. Answer all inquiries in an efficient and timely manner, allowing you to appease client concerns while simultaneously focusing on your daily tasks.

123 Main Street
September 1, 2020

When determining the value of a property, we look at the following core criteria to assess the proper placement of each particular property within its competitive marketplace:

1. Location
2. View
3. Lot Size
4. Square footage of structure
5. Condition
6. Desirability

Based upon recent sales activity and the current inventory of homes available, our estimation of value for the home at 123 Main Street is as follows:

Componentized Analysis

Approximate Structural Value:	square feet x $ per square foot	= $
Approximate Land Value:	square feet x $ per square foot	= $

Total Current Replacement Value = $

Depth of credible & willing buyers, improving overall market conditions, inventory levels, and general marketing statistics indicate, based upon the following list prices, you should anticipate the following marketing time for your property:

Prepared By:
John McMonigle

123 MAIN STREET
MARKET ANALYSIS
As Of 10/04/20

agent*inc.*

ADDRESS	SQ. FT.	$ PSF	LOT	BED	BATH	YEAR BUILT	PROPOSED LIST PRICE	ANTICIPATED SHELF LIFE
123 MAIN STREET	4,684	$0	5,600	3	4	1969		90 Days
123 MAIN STREET	4,684	$0	5,600	3	4	1969		180 Days
123 MAIN STREET	4,684	$0	5,600	3	4	1969		300 Days

Structure & Lot SF per both MLS & Realist

ACTIVE, BACK-UP & PENDING PROPERTIES

ADDRESS	SQ. FT.	$ PSF	LOT	BED	BATH	YEAR BUILT	CURRENT LIST PRICE	ORIGINAL LIST PRICE	% CHG	CDOM	TYPE
123 MAIN STREET	4,684	$0	5,600	3	4	1969			0%	264	active
123 MAIN STREET	4,414	$2,300	5,580	4	6	1973			0%	3	active
123 MAIN STREET	4,571	$2,430	6,000	3	4	1974			0%	25	active
123 MAIN STREET	4,571	$2,515	5,000	5	5	2020			0%	39	active
123 MAIN STREET	5,500	$4,909	5,700	4	5	2020			0%	91	active
AVERAGE	**$4,748**	**$2,431**	**$5,576**	**4**	**5**				**$0**	**84**	

SOLD PROPERTIES
2016 to Present

ADDRESS	SQ. FT.	$ PSF	LOT	BED	BATH	YEAR BUILT	SOLD PRICE	ORIGINAL LIST PRICE	CHG IN PRICE	CDOM	TYPE	COE
123 MAIN STREET	3,116	$2,968	7,003	4	5	1968				173	Standard	8/31/20
123 MAIN STREET	5,655	$1,450	8,708	4	5	1969				229	Standard	9/15/20
123 MAIN STREET	14,200	$0	22,461	6	12	1990				508	Standard	10/18/19
123 MAIN STREET	8,785	$0	8,276	5	7	1983				376	Standard	8/29/19
123 MAIN STREET	8,428	$0	10,090	5	8	2005				100	Standard	7/23/18
123 MAIN STREET	4,607	$0	4,856	4	5	1997				296	Standard	5/1/18
123 MAIN STREET	3,948	$0	7,550	4	5	1940				139	Standard	12/28/16
123 MAIN STREET	5,516	$0	6,591	5	5	1994				267	Standard	1/5/16
123 MAIN STREET	5,388	$0	8,450	4	6	1983				83	Standard	1/29/16
AVERAGE	**6,958**	**$491**	**8,331**	**5**	**7**					**238**		

2021 **AUGUST**
CALENDAR YEAR   CALENDAR MONTH

MONDAY
FIRST DAY OF WEEK

agent*inc.*

Monday	Tuesday	Wednesday	Thursday	Friday	Saturday	Sunday
26	30	31	01 Social Media Advertisement I PRESENTATION AT CDM NEW HOME FINDING CENTER	02 Social Media Advertisement I Planning for Agent Inc. Volume III editorial on condos	03 Social Media Advertisement I Retargeting Campaign Begins	04 Social Media Advertisement
05 Social Media Advertisement	06 Social Media Advertisement I Television Commercial Meeting	07 Social Media Advertisement	08 Social Media Advertisement I PRESENTATION AT ARIZONA NEW HOME FINDING CENTER	09 Social Media Advertisement I Television Commercial Meeting	10 Social Media Advertisement	11 Social Media Advertisement
12 Social Media Advertisement	13 Social Media Advertisement I Modern Luxury Ad Design	14 Social Media Advertisement I JUST LISTED E-CARD ORDER PLACED	15 Social Media Advertisement	16 Social Media Advertisement	17 Social Media Advertisement I Modern Luxury for September 1st Issue Order Placed with Modern Luxury	18 Social Media Advertisement
19 Social Media Advertisement	20 Television Ad BEGINS RUNNING - (DAILY)	21 Social Media Advertisement I Television Ad	22 Social Media Advertisement I Television Ad	23 Social Media Advertisement I PRESENTATION AT LA JOLLA NEW HOME FINDING CENTER	24 Social Media Advertisement I Television Ad	25 Social Media Advertisement I Television Ad
26 Social Media Advertisement I Television Ad	27 Social Media Advertisement I Television Ad	28 Social Media Advertisement I PRESENTATION AT RANCHO SANTA FE NEW HOME FINDING CENTER	29 Social Media Advertisement I Television Ad	30 Social Media Advertisement I Television Ad	31 Social Media Advertisement I Television Ad	01
02	03	04	05	06	07	08

9. **Provide professional marketing copy.**

Our marketing department is here to ensure that your brochures, advertisements, social media campaigns, and listings are designed to engage viewers, drive traffic, and generate leads. By providing your client with elite, professionally curated marketing materials, you will leave a lasting impression of your dedication to your craft and servitude that will translate into repeat clients and referrals.

The Agentinc. presentation box includes:

Elevated magazine
Marketing brochures
Listing presentation hardcover book
Comps
Sample marketing calendar
Hard-copy listing agreement
Sample postcards

Note for Agentinc. agents: All past marketing materials can also be found in the Agentinc. Collateral Closet.

You can also find the following samples:

Listing presentation (see AgentIncListingPresentation.co)
Elevated magazine (see ElevatedMagazine.co)

Mental Health Assessment ✑

0-1 doesn't match   2-3 partial match   4-5 strong match   x put check mark in the related box

I laugh at myself and with others.

| 0 | 1 | 2 | 3 | 4 | 5 |

I respect others, even if they have a different point of view.

| 0 | 1 | 2 | 3 | 4 | 5 |

I am able to accept life's disappointments.

| 0 | 1 | 2 | 3 | 4 | 5 |

Love Aspects To Focus On ✑   Recommended Reading ✑
Mental Health   A Blueprint for Success

Daily Schedule, Day 19. 🕐

AM	PM
06.00 His Word, First Word, Prayer	12.00
07.00 Exercise	01.00
08.00 Order Your Agent Inc. Presentation Box	02.00
	03.00
09.00 Prepare Your Listing Presentation	04.00
10.00	05.00
11.00	06.00 Home with Family
	07.00
	08.00 His Word, Last Word, Prayer

NETWORK WITH GATE GUARDS

Do to others as you would have them do to you. (NIV)

Luke 6:31

B y now you realize that acquiring listings is the key to your success. But listings aren't easy to gather—they certainly don't
grow on trees. But by using a program of love, gratitude, and dedication, you can easily expand your network and clientele.

What made me a successful agent in the early stages of my
career was my ability to think outside the box, especially when
it came to marketing and marketing channels. As you know, it is
important for you to have professionally designed marketing materials available in brochure or postcard form, as well as digitally on
websites and social media. While sending out mailers and working
to drive traffic to your website and social media accounts can be
beneficial, sometimes it takes a more direct marketing approach to
generate immediate results.

Like everything sales related, momentum and success in our
industry depend on leads, referrals, and quality of service. But
without a lead, there can be no referrals, and without leads, no one
will be able to experience your exceptional dedication to service.
That's why it is important to take some time to target specific areas

of your farm to create a pipeline of leads. One of the best ways to do this is by researching the gated communities in your farm and befriending the gate guards.

Gate guards are an untapped resource for leads. The people who work the gates are the eyes and ears of the entire community. They are on a first-name basis with their residents. They know the names of the residents' children and friends. They know the residents' likes, dislikes, birthdays, favorite sports, vacation spots, hobbies, and preferred restaurants. They care for these people on a daily basis and are familiar with who and what goes in and out of the community. This means they have access to vendor information—they know the popular pool cleaner, the builder responsible for the new add-on, the designer who crafted the custom wrought iron gate, the residents who are thinking about selling, and the residents who are thinking about buying a second home. By becoming acquainted with the gate guard, you can gain access to the social framework of an entire community of homeowners. By treating the gate guard with respect and friendship, you can place yourself in a position where you are just as important as every resident who passes through those gates each day.

Guard-gated communities make up a significant number of our communities. However, there are limitations to farming a guard-gated community. You typically will not have as much open house traffic. Open houses may be limited. Signage may be restricted and so on. Nevertheless, I have had my biggest successes in the exclusive and renowned coastal Orange County guard-gated communities of The Pelicans and Shady Canyon. I did it by making the guard gate attendants my friends and disciples. I made them a part of Team McMonigle.

"To have friends, you must show yourself friendly." I got to know the gate guards' names, laughed with them, joked with them, and brought them a nice open house list with my business card stapled to it every Friday for them to hand out on the weekends. They liked having this information handy because they would get frustrated when nonresidents drove up to inquire about open houses.

This way, they could be much more polite and professional and pass along my information.

It's not against any law to buy lead generation. Therefore, I made it my practice to have one-on-one conversations with each guard. I wanted them to call me on my cell phone in the following circumstances:

1. Any time a new agent was cleared through the gate to go to an address that was not actively listed
2. Any time a vacant home was being enhanced by sub-contractors
3. Any time someone was served an eviction
4. Any time an appraiser was cleared through the gate for a property not actively listed
5. Any time another agent entered to visit a new seller or one of my current listings

Most of these guards make around $25 per hour, which equates to about $4,000 per month before taxes. I was in the habit of giving them cash for lead generation and delivering it immediately.

I paid $50 in cash for a buyer's name and contact. These would usually come from members of the general public who pulled up to the gate and inquired. I paid $100 in cash for a tip on a seller whether anything came of it or not. When transactions closed, I would remember the procuring guard with a gift of $500. You do the math. These guys were incrementally increasing their pay and were completely loyal to Team McMonigle. Not much went on in that neighborhood that I didn't know about.

You might say, "Well, my farm is not guard-gated." That's okay. Sometimes you can develop a similar relationship with the people and residents who run the clubhouse. There are always influential people in each community whom you can get to be on your team.

Follow these important steps to network with the gate guard in your farm:

1. **Introduce yourself.**

   Introduce yourself in a friendly way to all the guards on duty. Do a little research and find the times when their shifts change. Show up at those times, and bring them a competitive market analysis with your card attached. Ask their names, find out their interests, and explain to them who you are and what you aim to accomplish in the community. Ask if you can leave marketing materials with them for anyone who might be interested in your service.

2. **Bring a gift.**

   Everyone loves gifts! Drop off cookies or a cold beverage for the guard when you're in the neighborhood. Bring a small something for their birthday. Deliver a gift card at Christmas. Explain how you'd love to help the community and assist anyone with finding household services and vendors, or selling their home. Your generosity will not go unnoticed. If the guard is impressed by your commitment to your craft, chances are they will spread the word.

3. **Ask about vendors.**

   Explain to the gate guard that you are a neighborhood expert and that you and your team are always looking for high-quality businesses to assist your clients. Create a list of popular vendors who work in the neighborhood and reach out to them for introductions and referrals.

4. **Follow up.**

   If one of your guards comes through with a lead, do not let a day go by without thanking them and dropping off something nice, like a gift card or bottle of wine. There's a lot of quid pro quo in real estate. When someone is generous enough to think of you and your livelihood, it is only right that you should return the generosity and continue to build and nurture a two-way relationship.

Emotional Health Assessment

0-1 doesn't match 2-3 partial match 4-5 strong match x put check mark in the related box

I am appreciative of others and think kindly of them.

0 ☐ 1 ☐ 2 ☐ 3 ☐ 4 ☐ 5 ☐

I am optimistic about my future.

0 ☐ 1 ☐ 2 ☐ 3 ☐ 4 ☐ 5 ☐

I support my friends and family in all of their endeavors.

0 ☐ 1 ☐ 2 ☐ 3 ☐ 4 ☐ 5 ☐

I am able to bounce back from disappointment.

0 ☐ 1 ☐ 2 ☐ 3 ☐ 4 ☐ 5 ☐

Love Aspects To Focus On
Emotional Health

Recommended Reading
A Blueprint for Success

Daily Schedule, Day 20.

AM		PM	
06.00	His Word, First Word, Prayer	12.00	
07.00	Exercise	01.00	
08.00	Introduce Yourself to the Gate Guard	02.00	
09.00		03.00	
10.00		04.00	
11.00		05.00	
		06.00	Home with Family
		07.00	
		08.00	His Word, Last Word, Prayer

NETWORK WITH HOTEL CONCIERGES AND WEALTH MANAGERS

Love one another with brotherly affection. Outdo one another in showing honor. (ESV)

Romans 12:10

Continuing with yesterday's lesson of friendship and networking within your farm, another untapped resource for lead generation via the path of love and gratitude can be found in your local hotels and resorts as well as local wealth managers.

For decades I have been able to turn my relationships with concierges at four- or five-star hotels into tangible real estate client opportunities. Just like the gate guard at your local gated community, the hotel concierge has access to a vast cache of potential real estate clients. As you know, part of the job of a concierge is to answer any and all questions about the neighborhood and region. Concierges know where to find the finest sushi restaurant, where to go for a romantic evening stroll, where to find the best surf, where to get a delectable craft cocktail, where to get a car serviced, and . . . who the best realtors in the area are.

Hotels consistently host people who are staying in the area looking to relocate, or who are remodeling their home, or who are having home troubles, or who are between homes, or who are looking for a second home—each of these guests is a potential client for you.

By simply stopping by your local hotels and resorts and asking if you can be of service, you will instill yourself not only in the memory of the concierge but also in the memories of those looking to buy or sell a home.

Here are a few pointers to get you in the door with your hotel concierge:

1. **Introduce yourself.**
   Introduce yourself to each concierge and explain who you are and what you do. More often than not, there will be a place to leave marketing materials for local services. Ask the concierge if you can leave some of your materials with them to assist anyone who is inquiring about real estate in the area. If there is a rack for local magazines, make sure to add a few of your personalized *Elevated* magazines to it, front and center. And of course, leave a stack of business cards with them for anyone who might be looking for help.

2. **Bring a gift.**
   Again, everyone loves gifts! Put a smile on your concierge's face while they're at work—I can guarantee they will remember you forever.

3. **Promise a finder's fee.**
   Everyone loves free money and an additional income opportunity.

4. **Sell your value proposition and specialty.**
   Let concierges know you are a specialist and a dedicated professional.

5. **Ask about vendors.**
   Hotels are a wealth of information about neighborhood vendors. Ask concierges about who the hotel uses for

maintenance and landscaping, and reach out to these vendors to ask if they would like to be added to your neighborhood specialist page.

6. **Follow up.**

Follow up every week to see if concierges need anything. Always have a suggestion for them—caterers, yacht charters, drivers, and so on. Be helpful. Again, if your hotel concierge sends a lead your way, repay them with gratitude immediately. Bring something special that will brighten their day.

7. **Leave behind marketing materials.**

Leave a comparative market analysis (CMA), an open house list, brochures from trusted vendors (concierges are always looking for these), flyers for any restaurant promotions you have created, and so on.

As you build these five to ten relationships, your phone will start to ring. Make it your goal to get your magazine into each room. Try to place your property videos on the in-room televisions. Drop by and say hello often. Always have a gift.

Networking with a Wealth Manager

"By showcasing your ability to manage a wealth manager's clients professionally and successfully, you will gain a lifelong ally who can trust you to deliver beneficial financial results."

This is big! Think of this person as your partner. Only have one, and choose the best. Connecting with a local wealth manager is a great way to generate leads and expand your clientele. Wealth managers are responsible for crucial financial decisions and are trusted to make the correct moves when it comes to their client's wealth, including real estate investments. By showcasing your ability to manage a wealth manager's clients professionally and successfully, you will gain a lifelong ally who can trust you to deliver beneficial financial results. Reach out to a local wealth manager and invite them to lunch or coffee. Explain to them that they can rely on you to manage their clients skillfully, and in return, you will refer their wealth management services to your clients. Include them in your magazine, plan events with them, and constantly think of ways to entertain them with dinners, coffees, golf, and so on. This is one of your most productive synergistic relationships. Make sure you have a clear understanding with each other and complete trust and reciprocation.

And again, always reward those who help further your career with a gift!

Emotional Health Assessment ✁

0-1 doesn't match   2-3 partial match   4-5 strong match   x put check mark in the related box

I make healthy choices for myself.

| 0 | 1 | 2 | 3 | 4 | 5 |

I make healthy choices in my relationships.

| 0 | 1 | 2 | 3 | 4 | 5 |

I am aware of my own self-judgment.

| 0 | 1 | 2 | 3 | 4 | 5 |

I notice upsetting emotions when they arise.

| 0 | 1 | 2 | 3 | 4 | 5 |

Love Aspects To Focus On ✁   Recommended Reading ✁
Emotional Health   A Blueprint for Success

Daily Schedule, Day 21. 🕐

AM	PM
06.00 His Word, First Word, Prayer	12.00 Lunch with Wealth Managers and Concierges
07.00 Exercise	01.00 Network with Local Concierges
08.00	02.00
09.00 Make Calls to Set Up Appointments and Lunches	03.00
10.00	04.00
11.00	05.00
	06.00 Home with Family
	07.00
	08.00 His Word, Last Word, Prayer

NETWORK WITH DIVORCE ATTORNEYS

Judge not, and you will not be judged; condemn not, and you will not be condemned; forgive, and you will be forgiven. (ESV)

Luke 6:37

D ivorce is a difficult process not only for husband and wife but also for children, friends, family, neighbors, and anyone else who provides love and support to the nucleus of a marriage. In a perfect world, each of us would find our true companion, our "soul mate," and our lives and love would continue to flourish and be nourished until the day we leave this magnificent world. Unfortunately, the reality is that divorce exists and it is something that affects us as agents every single day.

If we look to Scripture, it's obvious God is not supportive of divorce.

"For I hate divorce," says the Lord, the God of Israel, "and him who covers his garment with wrong," says the Lord of hosts. "So take heed to your spirit, that you do not deal treacherously." (NASB)

Malachi 2:16

This is a straightforward, easy to understand message. God is telling us that marriage is a divine institution and should be respected and upheld to the highest degree. Unfortunately, despite God's wishes, divorce is at a record high in our country and continuously threatens to destroy the very foundation of our society.

I myself never imagined I would end up divorced. I didn't realize divorce was something I had little control over. But God gave us all free will, the freedom to choose, right? I fought for years to keep my marriage and my family together. Still, in the end, I was left without a choice, and the inability to maintain my marriage crushed my soul and shattered my heart. To make matters worse, it caused my children to suffer from an extremely severe case of parent alienation. And as a parent, there is nothing worse than watching your children suffer.

As I began to pick up the pieces of my life, I came to understand that love and forgiveness are essential to our ability to overcome the suffering and alienation associated with divorce. Because of my own personal experience, I implore you to do everything you can to discourage divorce. If you have a friend in need, help them fight for their marriage. Believe that God has the power to transform hearts and create a better future, a future filled with love, renewed connection, and newfound appreciation. It is with this desire to serve and minister that you should approach all divorce cases when it comes to real estate.

In your career as an agent, you will represent clients who are going through a divorce. They may be working to sell their mutual home or trying to relocate separately. As an agent, you will likely witness a myriad of emotions on display during your client interactions. It's important to remember that when you are handling these delicate scenarios, you must first act as a Christian—you must provide service and guidance for clients during what is likely one of the most profoundly disruptive and stressful experiences they will ever have to endure in their lifetime. Compound their anxiety, fear, and sadness with the stress of finding, buying, or selling a home, and you have a recipe for an intense emotional landscape.

Because divorce is a fairly common reason for buying and selling, I have found over the years that my relationships with divorce attorneys have afforded me the opportunity to help guide clients through their extremely difficult financial and personal experiences. My ability to reach out to these attorneys allowed me to gain a reputation as an agent who could handle angry, warring, and emotionally exhausted clients. It allowed me to gain a reputation of being compassionate, honest, and efficient when handling these matters, and it opened up a pipeline of clients who simply wanted someone they could trust to do the heavy lifting during a fragile moment in their lives.

When you are looking to expand your clientele, it is wise to reach out to the divorce attorneys in your county, drop by their offices, offer to take them to lunch, and differentiate yourself as an agent who prioritizes their clients' emotions and demands first and foremost, and as someone who has the capacity to be fair, just, and professionally composed throughout the litigation and transactional process.

Now, not everyone is cut out to navigate the deep emotional chasm of a divorce client, but I can say with confidence that, as agents, we are in this industry to serve, and your willingness to learn to deal with uncomfortable client situations will allow you to grow both as an agent and as a servant of God. And, simply put, divorce attorneys can allow you to build your client base, while also providing you with the satisfaction of helping a fellow community member through a time of crisis.

In order to successfully network with your region's divorce attorneys, you must exhibit certain characteristics that indicate your ability to expertly manage their clients' expectations. Here are a few traits divorce attorneys look for in an agent:

1. **You are dedicated to service.**
   Above all else, you are an agent who is willing to work with people in their time of need to make their difficult lives easier.
2. **You know how to tackle the issues.**
   Understanding what each party expects and working to resolve any issues should be at the forefront of your approach to divorced clients.
3. **You are a calm and professional individual.**
   You need to demonstrate that you are able to pacify volatile clients with your insight and compassion.
4. **You are eager to give divorce attorneys a referral.**
   Business relationships are a two-way street. Providing your attorneys and anyone else in your network with referrals that lead to business is the best way to remain on their radar and receive your own referrals.

It is also important to note that you can pay the attorney a referral fee out of escrow, allowing you to provide monetary compensation for trusting you with the livelihoods of their clients. As with all relationships—including marriage—trust is a key component in creating a successful and long-lasting bond. Once you have demonstrated your value, your servitude, your gratitude, and your professionalism to an attorney, they will turn to you over the course of their career, knowing you are able to confidently and expertly provide real estate guidance for their clients, which in turn makes their job and their own client relationships easier to manage.

Emotional Health Assessment ✓

0-1 doesn't match   2-3 partial match   4-5 strong match   x put check mark in the related box

I do not judge others, and I accept their differences.

`0` `1` `2` `3` `4` `5`

I nurture my social connections.

`0` `1` `2` `3` `4` `5`

I learn from my mistakes.

`0` `1` `2` `3` `4` `5`

I cultivate kindness.

`0` `1` `2` `3` `4` `5`

Love Aspects To Focus On ✓   Recommended Reading ✓
Emotional Health   A Blueprint for Success

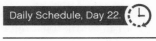

Daily Schedule, Day 22.

AM	PM
06.00 His Word, First Word, Prayer	12.00 Networking Lunch
07.00 Exercise	01.00
08.00	02.00
09.00 Make Calls to Set Up Appointments with Attorneys and Schedule Lunches	03.00
	04.00
10.00	05.00
11.00	06.00 Home with Family
	07.00
	08.00 His Word, Last Word, Prayer

SCHEDULE A CHARITY DRIVE

And I have been a constant example of how you can help those in need by working hard. You should remember the words of the Lord Jesus: It is more blessed to give than to receive. (NLT)

Acts 20:35

As Christians, we are called to serve our communities, to volunteer our time, and to give ourselves to those in need. Again, the career you have chosen is wholly based on service, and because of this, you are capable of creating a better future for those you work with. You can transform lives. You can instill a lifelong memory in the hearts and minds of your clients, and you can also become a positive force and voice in your community.

I believe it is important that we serve from the heart, that we are in it for the right reasons, and that we are "in it to win it." It's important that we roll up our sleeves and get ourselves a little bit dirty with the people and programs that we promote so that our passion and service are real. This is not a self-promotion gimmick. In fact, Jesus tells us that if we announce our good deeds, we have already received our reward. Be real and be passionate about how, who, and what you decide to serve in your community.

It is my recommendation that each agent hold one or two charity drives or community events each year to provide help and assistance to those in need as well as make a difference in their community and farm. One or two days a year of selfless giving can be a powerful tool to expand your neighborhood presence while also doing the work God expects of you for your neighbors.

Here are a few pointers for setting up your charity drive or community event:

1. **Select a cause everyone can get behind.**
   Feed the hungry. Collect toys for underprivileged children at Christmas. Walk for multiple sclerosis. Avoid causes that do not have the interests of those in need as their foundation.

2. **Use your neighborhood hashtag to generate attention.**
   No one likes failed philanthropic missions, especially those who are depending upon volunteers like you to help them in a difficult time. Use your marketing tools to raise awareness about your cause or event. Not only will you help those in need by reaching a greater audience, but you will also instantly connect with your neighborhood by showcasing your devotion to servitude.

"Community events are a great place to socialize, network, and make a lasting impression on influential members of a community."

---

3. **Be active.**
   Bring coffee, green juice, or refreshments to the event and pass them out to the volunteers. Introduce yourself and explain why you want to help. Much of your success is dependent upon your ability to connect with those around

you in real time. Community events are a great place to socialize, network, and make a lasting impression on influential members of a community.

4. **Plan a neighborhood garage sale and donate a percentage to charity.**

Everyone loves a neighborhood garage sale! Reach out to members of the homeowners association (HOA) in your farm and unite your community through a common goal. Neighborhood garage sales drive traffic directly to you and through you—this is especially useful if you have an open house coming up in the area. Ask around and see what charities your potential clients feel connected to, and donate a portion of the proceeds to the charity.

When your farm witnesses your willingness to sacrifice spare time to invest in their community, you are differentiating yourself, leading by example, and connecting with the most active members in the community, who can offer referrals to neighbors when they need a thoughtful, dedicated neighborhood specialist agent.

Emotional Health Assessment ✂

0-1 doesn't match   2-3 partial match   4-5 strong match   x put check mark in the related box

I practice forgiveness.

| 0 | | 1 | | 2 | | 3 | | 4 | | 5 | |

I am able to express my emotions in a positive manner.

| 0 | | 1 | | 2 | | 3 | | 4 | | 5 | |

I look to God for peace of mind.

| 0 | | 1 | | 2 | | 3 | | 4 | | 5 | |

Love Aspects To Focus On ✂   Recommended Reading ✂
Emotional Health   Christians in the Workplace

Daily Schedule, Day 23. 🕐

AM		**PM**	
06.00	His Word, First Word, Prayer	12.00	Networking Lunch
07.00	Exercise	01.00	
08.00	Research Charities that Interest You and Your Farm	02.00	
		03.00	
09.00	Make Calls to Set Up Appointments and Lunches	04.00	
10.00		05.00	
11.00		06.00	Home with Family
		07.00	
		08.00	His Word, Last Word, Prayer

VISIT HOA MEETINGS AND TRY TO JOIN AS A BOARD MEMBER

So in Christ we, though many, form one body, and each member belongs to all the others. (NIV)

Romans 12:5

B y now, you may be noticing a running theme behind *40 Days of Farming*—community presence. Your Christian dedication to activities that benefit your farm is directly related to generating leads and clients. There are several untapped resources for finding leads and clients in your farm if you know where to look. The HOAs in your neighborhood are a great resource for networking—they provide an opportunity to get to know your community, introduce yourself to prospective clients, and connect with vendors and services.

Almost one in every four homes across America is in an HOA. In Orange County, just about all of them are in an HOA. But how do you get involved in one of your neighborhood HOAs? Start by taking the time to write down the days and times of each HOA meeting occurring in your farm, and make a point to attend them. While at the meeting, you should take several important actions:

1. **Obtain a copy of the covenants, conditions, and restrictions (CC&R) and save it in your Agentinc. Geographic
   Farming Operations Manual or brokerage binder.**
   The CC&R will give you valuable information about the
   housing development, providing you with the knowledge
   necessary to become an expert on the neighborhood and its
   restrictions and limitations. Print out an updated copy of
   the CC&R and keep it. This can prevent a delay when a fast
   escrow is needed or simply be useful to answer questions.

2. **Meet the manager of the HOA. Introduce yourself as
   a specialist.**
   Ask to be included in all emails and notifications, and ask
   to receive all meeting schedules. It is important to know
   that you do not have to live within the HOA in your farm
   to become a board member. By becoming a board member, you give yourself access to a select group of individuals who deeply care about where they live and want only
   the best for the community's residents. Your willingness to
   assist in creating a safe, beautiful, and pleasant neighborhood exemplifies your dedication to your farm and to your
   community. These board members are likely the most vocal
   members of their development—getting to know them and
   helping them achieve their goals will give you access to the
   community's residents as well as cultivate intimate knowledge of market activity and vendors within it.

   "Again, your dedication, servitude, and presence
   in your community and farm will make a
   lasting impression on its residents."

   ---

3. **Ask for the budget and a printout of any pending litigation or assessments. Find out if there are any pending
   HOA foreclosures.**

This involvement will inform you of all proposed construction, developer activity, maintenance deficiencies, litigation, and HOA payment delinquencies, as well as provide you with many more tidbits of information that will put you on the scent of your next listing.

4. **Join the architectural design review committee.**
By joining the architectural design review committee, you will always be abreast of current building in the community and will gain access to information about teardowns, remodels, and rebuilds, allowing you to seek out opportunities and reach out to future clients and developers. In addition, by joining the architectural design review committee, you will be able to identify popular architects in the development. It's important to note that architects are the first to know about future building and developments, so knowing the architects gives you a head start on communicating with potential clients and a distinct advantage when it comes to securing a listing.

There is often controversy, bickering, and gossip in these meetings—especially design review meetings. Delays of multimillion-dollar projects can cause heated arguments and tension. Remember to always love everyone and set yourself apart by finding something good to say about each person and each project.

Once you've created a calendar of each HOA meeting in your farm, reach out to the board of directors and ask for a copy of the agenda before each meeting to ensure that you are informed of the topics beforehand. Again, your dedication, service, and presence in your community and farm will make a lasting impression on its residents. In real estate, generating an organic, word-of-mouth following is an important step in bolstering your digital and print marketing strategies and allows you to imprint yourself on the minds of a group of potential sellers and buyers.

Relational Health Assessment ✂

0-1 doesn't match   2-3 partial match   4-5 strong match   x put check mark in the related box

I maintain a positive relationship with my church and its members.

`0` `1` `2` `3` `4` `5`

I am an active participant in my Christian community.

`0` `1` `2` `3` `4` `5`

Love Aspects To Focus On ✂   Recommended Reading ✂
Relational Health   Christians in the Workplace

Daily Schedule, Day 24. 🕐

AM	PM
06.00 His Word, First Word, Prayer	12.00 Networking Lunch
07.00 Exercise	01.00
08.00	02.00
09.00 Make Calls to HOA for an Appointment and Information on Membership	03.00
	04.00 Attend HOA Meeting
10.00	05.00
11.00	06.00 Home with Family
	07.00
	08.00 His Word, Last Word, Prayer

PREPARE FOR YOUR OPEN HOUSE

Be prepared, and prepare yourself, you and all your companies that are assembled about you, and be a guard for them. (NASB)

Ezekiel 38:7

We open our hearts to God. We open our houses to God. When you welcome people, be they family, friends, or strangers, into your home, you hold yourself to a high standard of grace, hospitality, and companionship, just as God does when He calls us into His own home. As I've mentioned before, one of the most important aspects—if not the most important aspect—of being a successful agent is your commitment and ability to throw a successful open house. In order to do so, you must take several important steps leading up to that day to prepare yourself for the potential buyers, community members, future clients, and neighbors in your farm you will be connecting with.

In the days leading up to your open house, you should focus on your marketing platform and CRM, reaching out to as many potential buyers as you can and inviting them to see your new listing. It's important to note that you've been hired to sell your client's home because of your ability to influence and connect with potential buyers. If you throw an open house and only three people come, what does that say to your client and your farm about your commitment to selling? Your commitment to positively affecting the lives of your clients entails putting in the effort to give them the best possible outcome. And the best possible outcome when it comes to selling a home is providing your client with high market visibility.

My success as a real estate agent is defined by my commitment and ability to "win in the living room" while throwing an open house. I make sure to arrive early and knock on neighbors' doors, introducing myself as the agent in charge of selling the house, handing out business cards, and inviting them to visit. I ask permission to place signs in neighbors' yards, allowing me to advertise and network simultaneously. Each time I show, I make sure I have at least 20 signs in the ground for my farm to recognize, giving me the ability to expand my network and brand, reach future clients, and attract potential buyers. I tell clients, "I'll be at such and such address on Saturday from 12 to 5. Stop by and we can chat. You should see this house anyway." This alone brings traffic and energy to the open house. Remember, everyone is watching.

On the day I show a house, I devote my time to ensuring that the property is in the best order and condition that I can manage personally. I air out the rooms, vacuum, tidy up, rearrange furniture, make beds, hose down patios, light scented candles, and play relaxing music—I do anything I need to do to make sure the home I am representing looks and feels like the perfect home for my potential buyer. I also bring an iPad with sign-in software that feeds directly into my CRM, strategically place the iPad in an area where visitors can't avoid it, and require that everyone attending sign in. This allows me to not only follow up with interested people, but also reach out to new people in my farm who may have leads and referrals.

Becoming successful at holding an open house takes practice, dedication, and experience. There will be times, especially in the beginning, when your open house may not attract the traffic you believed it would—and that's all right. As we all know, it's important to learn from our mistakes. If you find yourself in this position, do not give up! Instead, sit down and ask yourself why you were unsuccessful. Is it because you didn't market well enough? Were you not prepared when attendees arrived? Did you reach out enough to your CRM and the neighbors surrounding the property? At the end of the day, grade yourself on your performance—and make the necessary changes for the next open house.

When it comes to a showing, preparation leads to results. Below you'll find valuable information to successfully complete an open house. If you dedicate yourself to being an expert on not only the property but also the neighborhood and its amenities, you will successfully attract potential buyers and build your clientele.

Here are some tips on preparing to hold an open house:

1. **Get busy on your social media, email, mailing, and digital advertising campaign.**

   This may seem like a no-brainer, but plenty of agents don't do enough marketing before they hold an open house—the result is a lackluster event with very few interested parties. If you put the necessary time, energy, and money into filling your open house, you will prove to your clients and potential clients that you have the connections, know-how, and network to ensure a sale.

2. **Target your demographic.**

   Knowing your farm and understanding your CRM can help save you time when holding an open house. The idea is to generate potential buyers who will actually buy the home you are inviting them to see. If your home is in a suburban area occupied primarily by families, get the message out to potential clients with children. If your listing is a one-bedroom loft in SoHo, target potential clients who don't need much space and enjoy urban living.

"The idea is to generate potential buyers who will actually buy the home you are inviting them to see."

---

3. **Communicate with your client.**

   Many clients can get a bit nervous about letting strangers walk through their home and enter rooms without them present. Make sure you and your client discuss expectations, guidelines, restrictions, and requirements before anyone sets foot inside. Knowing exactly what your client expects and is comfortable with can save you a ton of stress and time on open house day.

4. **Get your signs out early.**

   Placing a sign in the grass in the neighborhood one hour before holding your open house will not attract anyone. Walk the neighborhood and introduce yourself to neighbors, asking if you might place a sign in their yard. Make sure your signs are in the ground with plenty of lead time to ensure that passersby get the message and have ample time to reach out to any friends or family looking to purchase a home.

By failing to prepare, you are preparing to fail.

Benjamin Franklin

Open House/Broker Preview Checklist

	Property Address:		Email:	Phone:
T	Lender Participant:			
E	Escrow Participant:			
A	Title Participant:			
M	Other Host Participant:			
	Date:	Time:		

	OPEN HOUSE/BROKER PREVIEW CHECKLIST		
1	OPEN HOUSE/PREVIEW	FROM:	TO:
2	Approve and schedule open house/preview. Date: _____	Agent	Client
3	Schedule open house in MLS	Agent	MLS
4	Schedule open house on Zillow	Agent	Zillow
5	Plan open house/broker preview	Agent	Agent
6	Contact escrow, title, and lender for assistance	Agent	Escrow/Lender
7	Determine menu or snacks/drinks, if applicable	Agent	Admin
8	Reserve rental items, if applicable	Agent	Rental Company
9	Notify neighborhood guard house, if applicable	Agent	Security
10	Schedule coverage for open house/event	Agent	Your Team
11	Promote open house	Agent	Agent
12	Post event on social media: Instagram, Facebook, LinkedIn	Agent	Social Media
13	Email to your brokerage or team	Agent	Brokerage
14	Boost social media posts to surrounding neighborhood	Agent	Social Media
15	Mail postcard to surrounding neighborhood	Agent	Marketing
16	Walk flyer to surrounding neighborhood	Agent	Agent
17	Email to neighborhood with help of title company	Agent	Title
18	Consider promoting on Adwerx, YouTube, Google Ads	Agent	Adwerx
19	Consider text blast through Al Touch	Agent	Title
20	Send open house information to admin to place on list of OPENS	Agent	Admin*
21	Prepare list of active competition and recent solds in area in general price range	Agent	MLS
22	Prepare neighborhood and city statistics	Agent	RPR/Escrow
23	Prepare open house flyer, unless using property brochure	Agent	Marketing
24	Print full agent MLS listing of property for reference sheet	Agent	Agent
25	Use guest sign-in method	Agent	Agent
26	Bring candles and matches or lighter	Agent	Agent
27	Bring music source, if not available in house	Agent	Agent
28	If vacant, consider bringing paper towels, cleaning spray, trash bags, toilet paper	Agent	Agent
29	Post open house signs around the neighborhood	Agent	Agent
30	Arrive early to set up house	Agent	Agent
31	Turn on all lights, light candles, and set music	Agent	Agent
32	Have food and drink delivered, if applicable	Agent	Escrow/Lender
33	Display all brochures and stat sheets	Agent	Admin
34	Be set up and ready 10 minutes early	Agent	Agent
35	FOLLOW UP AFTER OPEN HOUSE/PREVIEW	FROM:	TO:
36	Clean up, turn off music, extinguish candles, lock doors and windows, set alarm	Agent	Agent
37	Pick up open house signs	Agent	Agent
38	Update seller and co-agent on traffic	Agent	Seller
39	Enter results in property activity calendar	Agent	Agent
40	Enter new prospects into your CRM	Agent	CRM
41	Call or send intro email to new prospects and schedule follow up on CRM tasks	Agent	CRM
42	SCHEDULE NEXT WEEK'S OPEN HOUSE!		

Relational Health Assessment ✁

0-1 doesn't match   2-3 partial match   4-5 strong match   x put check mark in the related box

I have confidence in and respect for the people I have relationships with.

`0` `1` `2` `3` `4` `5`

I consider other people's opinions and incorporate their views in my personal growth.

`0` `1` `2` `3` `4` `5`

Love Aspects To Focus On ✁   Recommended Reading ✁
Relational Health   Christians in the Workplace

Daily Schedule, Day 25. 🕐

AM	PM
06.00 His Word, First Word, Prayer	12.00 Networking Lunch
07.00 Exercise	01.00
08.00 Begin Open House Checklist	02.00
09.00	03.00
10.00	04.00
11.00	05.00
	06.00 Home with Family
	07.00
	08.00 His Word, Last Word, Prayer

HOLD YOUR OPEN HOUSE

He was faithful to the one who appointed him, just as Moses was faithful in all God's house. (NIV)

Hebrews 3:2

The home is a place of love, of safety, and of joy. It represents our family, our marriage, our relationships, and our children. It protects us from weather and brings us a sense of comfort and safety. The home generates memories, provides a place to entertain guests, and brings forth life. For many people, their home is their most important and priceless possession. And for many people, finding the perfect home will be the most important decision they will ever make—for all the reasons mentioned above.

Now that you have prepared for your open house, it's time to hold it! Take some time right now to visualize your guests and community entering your listing property. What will you say? How will you feel? Let these emotions run through you and allow your mind, body, and spirit to embrace the anxiety, hope, nervousness, happiness, and excitement associated with this day. Take a moment to visualize the perfect buyer. Where do they come from? What do they look like? What will they like most about this home? See yourself accepting an offer. Visualize the joyous conversation you will have with your client.

As I've stated before, holding an open house is one of the most, if not the most, important aspects of building your career and becoming a successful agent. Your practice and devotion to creating an ideal environment for your guests is essential to not only attracting the right buyer but also attracting your next listing. If you have dedicated yourself to perfecting your pitch and have spent the necessary time and resources on your marketing campaign, you will soon be able to reap the rewards of your labor.

By now, you've selected your wardrobe, sorted out your catering, purchased a scented candle (hopefully), and selected the tone, atmosphere, and sounds you feel will leave a lasting impression on each person who walks through the door. When you arrive at your listing, take a look at what you've already accomplished. You have been blessed with a listing. You have the opportunity to use the talents God gave you to change the lives of several people in an instant. Be proud of who you are as an agent—and as a Christian. Provide the same hospitality to those who visit your open house that you would to a friend in your own home. Listen to your guests' questions and answer them with love, hope, and faith in your heart. Understand their reservations and talk them through their concerns. Be an upstanding member of the community and provide your expert knowledge of your farm to enhance your guests' experience and gain their trust. Today is not just about selling your listing—it is about enhancing your visibility, showcasing your talents, and creating an environment that represents your dedication to your career. This is your time to shine—let the community know you are here and that you are the best at what you do!

———————

"Be an upstanding member of the community and provide your expert knowledge of your farm to enhance your guests' experience and gain their trust."

———————

A successful open house is an art form and that's why no two agents do it the exact same way. But there are some core fundamentals that you should try to incorporate:

1. **Stay in control.**

   Why is this so important? Your seller expects you to have control of this asset. Potential buyers won't respect you if you don't.

   People actually admire a person who can gracefully set boundaries and guide an experience. I think of my trainer at the gym. I probably know as much as, or more than, he does about fitness, but for an hour I can go and relax my mind and trust he will maximize my training and protect me from injury.

   Customers want to meet you and feel comfortable that you know what you are doing. This way, they can relax and let you guide them. So setting some boundaries or guidelines at the front door in a kind and gracious way is important.

2. **Be welcoming and warm.**

   Celebrity Greeting

   Your greeting is key. Visitors are going to like you or question you in the first 15 seconds. I've heard agents say, "You know, I just like to sit over here and give them space and let them roam through the house." Good luck with that.

   Instead, give guests a celebrity greeting. Why do I use the word *celebrity*? Because that's how I want you to think about your performance. This is your hour of power! You are onstage! Listing someone's home is a very high calling. It is an incredible honor to be handed a family's most important and valuable asset. To successfully compete for that honor, you need to perform in the public domain. You are like a politician shaking hands and kissing babies. I don't say "think of yourself as a celebrity" because I think you should be narcissistic; I say it to give you a perspective on how you should intentionally show up. Sports teams drill for months before their first game. For the opportunity to make seven-figure incomes, we need to polish up and present. We need to practice in the mirror and perfect our greeting, eye contact, and voice tone.

Atmosphere and Ambience
I encourage you to pretend you are the manager of a new Hermès store. It is your job to make sure the lighting, music, scented candles, and beverage service are all perfectly in order and that every corner of the store is clean and organized before you open the doors.

3. **Be effective.**
What are your goals? Getting guests to sign in with contact info is your number one goal. You do this at the front door. You must position yourself in the control zone, place your iPad in a strategic location, and you must not let them get by you. Otherwise you are wasting your time.

Connect

People do business with people they like. So, while you're body blocking at the control zone, you must also be charming and personable.

Watch your guests sign in, and comment on their addresses. Ask questions, find commonality, serve them food, and most important, pitch a deal—this will save you weeks.

Be at the control zone when they leave, and ask a few questions:

1. My seller would like to know what you like about the house.
2. Are you working with an agent? Would you like to take my card?
3. Please accept my gift of our quarterly magazine and some local comps. Would you like to receive our digital magazine in your email?

Follow Up

Before you close down, email and call your seller to let them know how it went. Be accountable for what went wrong and what could have been done better.

Enter the contact info and feed it into your CRM. Set up the contacts for an auto drip campaign. Choose the top five to email and call before you leave. This immediate action can cement enthusiasm for a new relationship. Remember, your ability to provide elevated service can be a major differentiator for potential clients.

Relational Health Assessment ✁

0-1 doesn't match   2-3 partial match   4-5 strong match   x put check mark in the related box

I do my best to help those in need.

`0` `1` `2` `3` `4` `5`

I am respectful in my personal and professional relationships.

`0` `1` `2` `3` `4` `5`

Love Aspects To Focus On ✁
Relational Health

Recommended Reading ✁
Christians in the Workplace

Daily Schedule, Day 26. 🕐

AM	PM
06.00 His Word, First Word, Prayer	12.00
07.00 Exercise	01.00
08.00 Hold Your Open House	02.00
09.00	03.00
10.00	04.00
11.00	05.00
	06.00 Home with Family
	07.00
	08.00 His Word, Last Word, Prayer

Day 27

BEGIN POSTING AS A NEIGHBORHOOD SPECIALIST

How will they preach unless they are sent? Just as it is written, "How beautiful are the feet of those who bring good news of good things!" (NASB)

Romans 10:15

Spread the good news—of your community knowledge! In order to successfully integrate into your community and infuse value into it, you must immerse yourself in the interests, businesses, events, and amenities of your farm. Remember, your job as an agent is to help your clients with one of the biggest transactions of their lifetimes. Many of them view buying and selling a home as both momentous and extremely stressful. In order to gain the trust and respect of the clients in your farm, you must first demonstrate your dedication and knowledge of your area. One of the easiest ways to increase visibility and distinguish yourself as a neighborhood specialist is to begin posting on your neighborhood specialist page. Now, many people think social media posting is a tiresome act that reaps few to no rewards. This isn't true. Not only does your regular posting remind people in your farm that you are an engaged member of the community, but it also establishes valuable search engine optimization (SEO) for you and your brokerage, which increases web traffic to your website and social media pages.

You may think posting is a tedious and time-consuming exercise—but it shouldn't be. In fact, your posts should be short, fun, intriguing, and informative, and should never exceed 500 words for websites and should remain under 125 characters for social media. You can choose from an array of topics, including neighborhood events, holidays, business openings, building developments, safety, dining, happy hour, fish tacos—the list goes on and on. Just remember to keep your topics professional, upbeat, and positive. The people reading your posts are proud of where they live, and the potential clients moving into your farm may be "excited yet unsure" about what the neighborhood will be like once they finally arrive.

If writing isn't your strong suit, don't worry. You can reach out to our marketing team and we can provide you with copywriters who can assist you with your content. But for those of you who want to venture out on your own literary journey, here are a few tips to get you started:

"Create a list of questions your readers might ask,
and then answer them, one post at a time."

---

1. **Provide solutions to problems.**
   When it comes to real estate, most people are looking for answers to questions they don't have the answer to, like "What renovations are most valuable?" "What are the best schools?" and "How do I handle multiple offers?"

   Create a list of questions your readers might ask, and then answer them, one post at a time. If you can create useful, rich content, you will attract readers and drive traffic.

2. **Write for the web.**

   Nowadays, no one has time to read through pages and pages of information. We want things short and sweet, and we want answers to be easy to find. Come up with an engaging title for your post, and make sure all the important information is placed at the beginning of the article. Remember, this isn't a novel. It's okay to answer the question your readers are looking for at the very beginning and then circle back to the "why" behind it.

3. **Include pictures.**

   We are a visual society. Adding graphs, stats, and captivating photos immediately sets a tone for readers and engages them before they read the first sentence. Pictures are also a great opportunity to showcase the work you've done and the homes you've found and sold in your farm; they allow potential clients to develop a tangible connection to your abilities as an agent.

4. **Focus on your neighborhood.**

   Don't get off-topic. Establish yourself as a neighborhood specialist by discussing topics specific to your farm.

5. **Write for real estate agents as well as clients.**

   It's tempting to focus solely on attracting sellers and buyers with your posts—but it's also important to say something worthwhile that will pique the interest of other real estate agents. If agents outside your farm are impressed with the dedication and knowledge you display in your posts, they are more likely to refer potential clients to you as well as join Agentinc.

6. **Post regularly.**

   Consistently post content. This allows readers to rely on new information on a daily, weekly, or biweekly basis and also displays your professionalism and organization.

7. **Strike up a conversation.**

   One of the main goals of your posts should be to generate a two-way conversation between yourself and your potential clients. Ask questions, encourage comments, and strike up discussions with your readers. The more human you are, the greater visibility and positivity you create within your farm.

8. **Build relationships with other real estate influencers and posters.**

Reach out to other Agentinc. or real estate posters on social media. You have access to one of the largest and most interactive real estate networks in the country. By sharing the words of other agents and real estate influencers, you are actively supporting your own industry and opening yourself and your colleagues up to referrals, greater SEO visibility, and the expansion of your brand behind Agentinc. or your brokerage's messaging.

Relational Health Assessment

0-1 doesn't match   2-3 partial match   4-5 strong match   x put check mark in the related box

I do not expect others to change.

| 0 | 1 | 2 | 3 | 4 | 5 |

I use my faith to connect with others.

| 0 | 1 | 2 | 3 | 4 | 5 |

Love Aspects To Focus On
Relational Health

Recommended Reading
God's Power to Change Your Life

Daily Schedule, Day 27.

AM

06.00 His Word, First Word, Prayer

07.00 Exercise

08.00 Research Topics for Blog

09.00

10.00 Write Blog

11.00

PM

12.00 Networking Lunch

01.00

02.00

03.00

04.00

05.00

06.00 Home with Family

07.00

08.00 His Word, Last Word, Prayer

AWARD A RESIDENT OF YOUR FARM A PRIZE IN THE "HASHTAG OF THE MONTH" CONTEST

But thanks be to God, who gives us the victory through our Lord Jesus Christ. (ESV)

1 Corinthians 15:57

Everyone loves winning a contest! As we touched upon a couple of days ago, I recommend launching a social media contest based on the neighborhood hashtag you created. The contest can be anything from "Best Neighborhood Picture of the Week" to "Best Poem" to "Sunset of the Month." It's entirely up to you. The point of your contest is to generate interest in your neighborhood hashtag, gain followers, and increase impressions, which will result in greater visibility and lead generation.

However, if you don't have many followers, your post most likely won't generate many leads for you. If that's the case, reach out to your CRM and set up an email that introduces both your social media handle and the upcoming contest. In this email, you should:

1. Announce yourself as the neighborhood specialist.
2. Explain you are driving community awareness and connectivity through the use of the hashtag.
3. Encourage residents in your farm to use #yourfarm whenever they are celebrating a holiday, a birthday, or any other occasion or event that takes place in the community.
4. Let residents know you will be posting charity drives, community events, and future contests and giveaways through the hashtag.
5. Tell residents to follow your social media account to stay up-to-date on everything happening in the neighborhood.

Once you've established your neighborhood hashtag strategy, reach out to a local vendor regarding the prize, and ask if they'd like to be showcased in the hashtag contest. If they agree, ask if they might help you get the word out. For a local vendor, this is a great way to receive free marketing, a guaranteed sale or service, and the opportunity to highlight their business. Remember, generating business and buzz for the vendors in your farm will eventually lead to referrals.

"By facilitating community growth that flows directly through your social media channel, you are organically developing a valued presence within your farm, virtually."

So go out and have a little fun on social media. By facilitating community growth that flows directly through your social media channel, you are organically developing a valued presence within your farm, virtually. Know that by spending $25 or $50 or $100 on a prize for a resident of your farm, you are investing in the opportunity to make thousands of dollars down the road. By bringing joy to your community, you are once again establishing yourself as a steward dedicated to the growth of each and every resident.

Relational Health Assessment ✂

0-1 doesn't match   2-3 partial match   4-5 strong match   x put check mark in the related box

I continuously invest in my relationship with God.

0 ☐ 1 ☐ 2 ☐ 3 ☐ 4 ☐ 5 ☐

I am devoted to being an ambassador and unifier of my community.

0 ☐ 1 ☐ 2 ☐ 3 ☐ 4 ☐ 5 ☐

Love Aspects To Focus On ✂   Recommended Reading ✂
Relational Health   God's Power to Change Your Life

Daily Schedule, Day 28. 🕐

AM		PM	
06.00	His Word, First Word, Prayer	12.00	Networking Lunch
07.00	Exercise	01.00	
08.00	Establish #Hashtag Strategy	02.00	
09.00		03.00	
10.00	Create Social Media Content	04.00	
11.00		05.00	Announce Winner of #Hashtag of the Month Contest
		06.00	Home with Family
		07.00	
		08.00	His Word, Last Word, Prayer

And whatever you ask in prayer, you will receive, if you have faith. (ESV)

Matthew 21:22

Days
29-40

ESTABLISH A DIRECT MAIL
MARKETING CAMPAIGN

Sing to the Lord, all the earth! Announce every day how He delivers. (NET)

1 Chronicles 16:23

As an agent and a Christian, you know that communication is one of the most important aspects of your profession and faith. But how do you, as an agent and a Christian, communicate across a multitude of channels and platforms, allowing your brand, your business, and your spirit to represent and inspire your farm's collective consciousness? One excellent way to expand your reach, your brand, and your message is through an organized and cost-efficient direct mail marketing campaign. Now, I know what many of you are thinking: "No one reads the mail anymore." Sure, our mail is filled mostly with bills and junk and coupons—but that doesn't mean your face, your name, and your accomplishments as an agent don't deserve to be in someone's mailbox. I have always said, "I am not sure which half of my marketing is not working." Meaning that the more we do, the more we seal our future success. Today, many companies and agents have stopped direct mailing. This is the opportunity. Due to the lack of competition, you can now stand out by putting together a very simple yet consistent campaign.

When it comes to direct mail marketing, many agents are discouraged by two things: First, it costs money. Second, they expect their mail marketing to lead directly to a sale, and when it doesn't, they get discouraged. While it does cost money to send mail and not every mailer will lead to a sale, mail is still an important aspect of your marketing campaign. So let me dispel any anxiety you may have about this practice.

Let's start with costs. In order to create an effective mail marketing campaign, you need to understand that in our industry you must spend money to make money—but you don't have to spend a ton to generate results. At Agentinc., our marketing Resource Center has multiple templates for you to choose from for free. We give you all the tools you need to create a successful mail marketing campaign, including postcards, newsletters, and holiday blasts. It's important to note that you don't need to send marketing materials out every day, or even every week. Instead, send out postcards when you have a particular listing that represents the quintessential property in your farm. Then send another postcard when that property sells, letting your farm know that you are both capable and successful. Understand that the purpose of your mailer isn't to make a million dollars off a listing—it is to create name and brand recognition in your farm, which will eventually lead to a larger network of clients to engage and work with.

Which leads me to the second objection: mail marketing doesn't lead directly to income. Many agents start their mail marketing campaign and give up shortly thereafter because they see it as a waste of money—in other words, they believe their mailer will elicit a direct response that will bring in immediate income. But to understand the purpose of marketing in general, we must look at it from a macro level—that is to say, we aren't as concerned with getting a direct response or sale as we are with establishing trust, brand recognition, and name recognition. Once you have successfully instilled your brand into the zeitgeist of your farm, your life as an agent will become easier. Think of it this way: with a mail marketing campaign, the next time you're at your local coffee shop and you strike up a conversation with a fellow patron, the chance of being recognized becomes greater. With an engaging mail marketing campaign, the next time you call a potential client, there's a greater chance they've learned about your recent success. Your mail campaign allows clients to place confidence in your expertise and professionalism because you have invested the time, money, and resources to let them know of your presence and capabilities.

To get your mail marketing program started, I've put together a list of five simple steps to help build brand recognition:

1. **Design a listing postcard.**
    Each time you acquire a listing that typifies the culture and market of your farm, send out a notification alerting residents. Remember, people want to work with agents they believe are successful. Your ability to represent listings and showcase your dedication to a professional marketing campaign is a major differentiator.

2. **Announce your most recent sale.**
    As soon as you sell a property, let your farm know! Again, success leads to success. Be proud of your accomplishments and those around you will be proud as well. As a result, they will look to you for their own success.

3. **Select a newsletter template and send content to the residents of your farm.**
    It's a fact—people love stats and easy-to-access information. Let your residents know how much their neighbors' homes are selling for, with comps and dates of sale. Add a personalized message that touches upon the issues and concerns of the neighborhood, and try to highlight a local business to let your readers know you are dedicated to and

supportive of your farm. Our Agentinc. Media Department and Resource Center has access to several ready-made templates to help you design a newsletter that will give residents in your farm access to the information they need to make wise choices.

"When clients are looking to an agent to help them make one of the biggest decisions of their life, they expect the service of someone who is willing to do anything to ensure success."

---

4. **Keep your marketing materials consistent and on-brand.** Many agents get carried away with adding too much information in their mailers, which bores potential clients. Don't think of your marketing materials as a way to explain the industry or yourself in a thousand words. Instead, think of your mailers as a way to establish a visual connection to your brand. Use your image and your tagline to draw attention, and use the properties you represent as a clear representation of your message. Keep your colors and font uniform and establish an aesthetic that can be recognized upon first glance.

5. **Be consistent.** As with posting, sending marketing materials to your farm on a regular basis demonstrates your dedication to both your craft and your career. When clients are looking to an agent to help them make one of the biggest decisions of their lives, they expect the service of someone who is willing to do anything to ensure success. Your willingness to spend hard-earned pay on keeping your community informed speaks volumes.

Financial Health Assessment +

0-1 doesn't match   2-3 partial match   4-5 strong match   x put check mark in the related box

I value my partnership with God, both personally and professionally, each day.

| 0 | 1 | 2 | 3 | 4 | 5 |

I appreciate what I have and give what I have to those in need.

| 0 | 1 | 2 | 3 | 4 | 5 |

Love Aspects To Focus On +
Financial Health

Recommended Reading +
God's Power to Change Your Life

Daily Schedule, Day 29.

AM	
06.00	His Word, First Word, Prayer
07.00	Exercise
08.00	Design Postcard
09.00	Announce Recent Sales
10.00	Begin a Newsletter
11.00	

PM	
12.00	Networking Lunch
01.00	
02.00	
03.00	
04.00	
05.00	
06.00	Home with Family
07.00	
08.00	His Word, Last Word, Prayer

THE IMPORTANCE OF DELEGATION

Do not be anxious about anything, but in everything by prayer and supplication with thanksgiving let your requests be made known to God. (ESV)

Philippians 4:6

As an agent, you wear a lot of hats. When you're starting out on your path toward financial success in the real estate industry, it's easy to find yourself becoming buried in tasks that seemingly take away from your focus—acquiring listings. The day-to-day responsibilities of becoming a top agent require an inordinate amount of time—time that is seemingly impossible to find. That's why it is important to not only stick to a strict and organized schedule to efficiently manage time but also learn to delegate your responsibilities to third parties, colleagues, and team members.

It's easy for us as agents to find a comfort zone—just enough listings to get by, just enough buyers to pay our own mortgage. But to remain successful in real estate, it is absolutely essential for us to continue to expand our business, grow our network, and generate more leads and income. Now, I understand that one of the perks of being an agent is the control we have over our careers, our futures, and our livelihoods. But as you grow with Agentinc. or another brokerage, you will find that your ability to release control and to let go of micromanaging your own career will become beneficial in the long run.

But how can you release control? How can you continue to grow if you aren't involved in each minute aspect of every transaction you are in the process of completing? The answer is simple—delegate your responsibilities and trust in your partnership with God.

I started in this business as an assistant on a team. We were a fine-tuned machine. We all knew our responsibilities and were held accountable. The leader of that team was a retired basketball coach and he ran a successful real estate team well before real estate teams became popular. I learned a lot from this structure and carried many of the organizational principles forward as I grew my own sales career.

Henry Ford taught us that dividing labor leads to efficiency.

Great wealth is generated by leveraging labor underneath you. The trick is managing it and making it all go smoothly.

For several years in a row, the *Wall Street Journal* reported that Team McMonigle was the number one real estate team in the world. During those years, my small team was cranking through about $550M of gross sales per year. I could never have built a machine to service one of the toughest and most demanding luxury markets and customer bases in the world without knowing what I should delegate and to whom.

"Again, establishing a relationship with colleagues
you respect and admire is essential."

On average, I wanted to focus on making three listing presentations per day, driving and overseeing the marketing, being

involved in critical negotiations, and closing deals. This left a tre-
mendous number of tasks to be done by my talented team. We had
checklists and strict real time, streamlined reporting—and I must
say our service and communication were platinum.

I have noticed throughout my career that many agents strug-
gle to delegate anything. By being so hands-on, not only do they
give up a lot of freedom and flexibility, but they also may hurt their
own results. If you think about it, a showing or meeting cannot
happen if that agent has a hair or doctor appointment or is trying
to be with family or take a day off. In the end, this approach hurts
the client.

One of the most important relationships for an agent to cultivate in this industry is the one with their transaction coordinator.
Building a solid relationship with your TC will undoubtedly free up
time and allow you to focus on the main goal of your job—signing
clients. A good TC can help you immensely prior to escrow by handling purchase offers, taking care of preliminary title information,
fielding counteroffers, and expediting responses to clients. Think
of your TC as an assistant. They save you time in the field—and
any time saved allows you to grow your business. That said, you
may be asking yourself where you can find a solid, experienced TC
with the ability to multitask and elevate your business and brand.
Again, establishing a relationship with colleagues you respect and
admire is essential. Ask your fellow agents and escrow officers who
they recommend. Once you've acquired solid recommendations,
reach out to the TC who fits your future goals, and explain what
you expect from them. Tell them you need someone who is available after hours for contracts, DocuSigns, disclosures, and checklists, and ask if they can accommodate your business requirements.
Sometimes, you may find you'll have to pay them a little extra to
complete the tasks that require special attention—and that's fine.
By expanding their income, you will gain a meaningful member of
your team who can help create margin in your schedule. By nurtur-
ing a personal and professional relationship with your TC, you will

be able to focus more on your clients—the most important aspect of your career.

Remember, being a successful agent isn't just a singular journey. Your career affects the lives of many people around you—your clients, your vendors, your colleagues, and most of all, your family. Your ability to delegate tasks will allow you to work a schedule that satisfies your commitments, giving you the freedom and pleasure of spending time with those you cherish most.

Financial Health Assessment ✦
0-1 doesn't match   2-3 partial match   4-5 strong match   x put check mark in the related box

I am fair, just, and honest in my business dealings.

[0] [1] [2] [3] [4] [5]

I use my money to express worship and support my faith through tithing.

[0] [1] [2] [3] [4] [5]

Love Aspects To Focus On ✦   Recommended Reading ✦
Financial Health   God's Power to Change Your Life

Daily Schedule, Day 30. 🕐

AM		**PM**	
06.00	His Word, First Word, Prayer	12.00	Networking Lunch
07.00	Exercise	01.00	
08.00	Select Tasks You Can Delegate	02.00	
09.00		03.00	
10.00	Delegate Tasks to Your Core Support Team	04.00	
		05.00	
11.00		06.00	Home with Family
		07.00	
		08.00	His Word, Last Word, Prayer

BEGIN LOOKING FOR
AN ASSISTANT

Carry each other's burdens, and in this way you will fulfill the law of Christ. (NIV)

Galatians 6:2

As I've mentioned before, it's a common problem for agents to mismanage their time and focus their energy on aspects of the industry that do not bring in clients or income. In my experience, my ability to successfully manage my time allowed me to expand my network and acquire listings. But successfully managing your time takes a team. Many of you may think to yourselves that assistants are reserved only for the "top agents" in a region. You may think that an assistant isn't worth the financial investment—after all, you've been doing all the work yourself this long, so why shell out money for a little help?

When I first started in the business, my first broker pulled me aside and said to me, "Wear a nicer suit than you can afford, wear a nicer watch than you can afford, and drive a nicer car than you can afford." This is not my advice to you, but why was he telling me this? Because it takes an investment in your future to bring about the success you dream of.

What if instead of receiving a salary your assistant or "team member" participates in the entire cycle of a listing?

Let's say they do the following:

- Input MLS data
- Manage signs
- Coordinate photography
- Handle all first showings
- Manage the database
- Perform marketing inspections
- Manage repair requests
- Help with open houses
- Handle broker previews

Would all that be worth sharing 20 to 30 percent of each listing commission? Would that give you more time to generate new listings? If it's easier, start with a part-time assistant who can complete the above tasks and then when you can afford to do it, hire a full-time executive assistant to take care of the following:

- Schedule your calendar
- Pull your voicemails and read your emails
- Coordinate payables with your bookkeeper
- Run errands

"The amount of time we spend gathering listings and being present in our farm is directly linked to our success."

As we grow as real estate agents, we are expected to provide more for our clients. This includes marketing, accessibility, information, and of course, time. You have chosen a career path that requires an immense amount of attention to detail, knowledge, communication skills, and tireless effort. An assistant enables you to focus your attention on your clients, provide the accessibility necessary to successfully retain your clients, and continue to use the majority of your time to expand your network, instead of getting bogged down with the everyday responsibilities of establishing and managing your business. In my experience, it's best to hire someone you trust as soon as you feel you are financially capable of sharing a commission with them.

That said, an assistant doesn't need to cost you money. Many agents are just starting out, or restarting, and don't have listings of their own. By offering a new agent a position as your assistant and working together, you can successfully manage your time, while allowing them to expand their network and experience by helping you put up signs, throw open houses, establish marketing campaigns, and do outreach. Give your assistant the opportunity to grow by allowing them to manage buyers both inside and outside your farm, permitting you to focus your time on accruing listings. Incentivize their work by offering them 50 percent of the commission on a purchase.

Think of your business as the kitchen at your favorite restaurant. The chef isn't the only one making the salad, shucking the oysters, grilling the steak, and plating the desserts. It takes a team to pull together an amazing meal and build a brand. In this same way, you must trust that an assistant is an essential tool to your business development. The amount of time we spend gathering listings and being present in our farm is directly linked to our success. Simply stated, your time is best served finding listing clients to represent. By hiring an assistant to help create a margin in your schedule to focus on this singularly essential task, you are making an important and vital personal and financial investment in a more lucrative future.

Financial Health Assessment ✦
0-1 doesn't match   2-3 partial match   4-5 strong match   ✕ put check mark in the related box

I save money when I can and use it to promote happiness for those around me.

0️⃣ 1️⃣ 2️⃣ 3️⃣ 4️⃣ 5️⃣

I use my money to create more opportunity for myself and for God, my partner.

0️⃣ 1️⃣ 2️⃣ 3️⃣ 4️⃣ 5️⃣

Love Aspects To Focus On ✦   Recommended Reading ✦
Financial Health   God's Power to Change Your Life

Daily Schedule, Day 31. 🕐

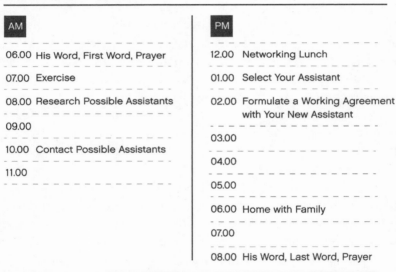

AM

06.00	His Word, First Word, Prayer
07.00	Exercise
08.00	Research Possible Assistants
09.00	
10.00	Contact Possible Assistants
11.00	

PM

12.00	Networking Lunch
01.00	Select Your Assistant
02.00	Formulate a Working Agreement with Your New Assistant
03.00	
04.00	
05.00	
06.00	Home with Family
07.00	
08.00	His Word, Last Word, Prayer

20 CALLS AND 10 BUSINESS CARDS EVERY DAY

Do not let any unwholesome talk come out of your mouths, but only what is helpful for building others up according to their needs, that it may benefit those who listen. (NIV)

Ephesians 4:29

God calls upon us to reach out to those in need. It is our duty as Christians and as agents to do our very best to be of service to our communities, to lead by example, and to dedicate ourselves to our faith and our chosen career paths wholly and universally. Remember, God is renting us our bodies, our intellect, and our willingness to succeed. When we are given an opportunity to change the lives of not only ourselves but also others in a positive way, we must respect this gift by putting forth the necessary amount of effort to realize its potential.

Your dedication to communication is vital to your success as an agent. Your ability to reach and connect with the people in your farm is one of the most important ways you can generate clients and change lives. That is why for as long as I've been an agent, I have disciplined myself to make 20 calls a day to colleagues, friends, and residents in my farm to generate leads and showcase my commitment to my craft and my community. I have always said, "If you aren't on the phone, you're not making money."

If you've been religiously adding to your AI Touch CRM, you should have hundreds or thousands of people you can immediately contact and establish a relationship with—so finding 20 people to call every day should be easy! Getting started is simple. Set up a priority list in your AI Touch CRM, block out one hour a day, and make 20 calls. With AI Touch, you can create notes for each of your contacts, keep track of your daily outreach, and schedule follow-ups, all with the click of a button.

But it's not just about making a phone call—it's about your ability to connect with prospective clients on a personal and professional level and gain their trust and business. In order to help you achieve this goal, I've put together a few tips:

1. **If you have a mutual friend or common interest, discuss this up front.**
   We interact with hundreds of people each day without even knowing it. The smallest connection between an agent and a prospective client can turn a cold call into a hot lead. Call the parents of the kids your children go to school with. Connect with your favorite chef. Reach out to the owners of your favorite shops. All of these people know people who know people—and there's always someone looking for an agent's help.

2. **Ask people if they are currently working with another agent. Ask if they would consider working with you instead.**
   If they say yes, great—you've just landed a client! If they say no, continue moving forward. As you know, referrals are directly linked to your success as an agent. Ask if they

know anyone who might need assistance. Even if they say no, they will remember your offer the next time they know someone who is looking for an agent.

3.   **Gather contact information.**

Make sure you have the correct information for your contacts in your CRM. If you receive a referral, enter the information immediately and reach out as soon as possible.

4.   **Follow up.**

Good business requires a commitment not only to initial outreach but also to the follow-up call, email, or mailer. Even if you've landed a client, it is important to keep them up-to-date and informed on what is happening in their community. Send them recent listings and comps—this information may inspire them to list. This is the time to showcase your work ethic to your farm. Once your referral turns into a client and you have successfully assisted them, follow up again and ask them for a referral.

5.   **Don't just call potential clients—call potential agents.**

As you know, Agentinc.'s revolutionary Revenue Share Program awards you for each agent you bring aboard. By devoting some of your call time to agents and colleagues who are a good fit for Agentinc., you are increasing your passive income between listings, allowing you to continue focusing on your future goals as an agent.

6.   **Don't give up.**

It's easy to say, "I made 20 calls today. Now, when do I get clients?" But 20 calls are just the beginning. These 20 calls may lead to an additional 20 calls that lead to hot leads. Or these 20 calls may lead to nothing. Eventually, your ability to insert yourself into the collective consciousness of your market will separate you from your competition and lead to a larger network to pull from.

To assist you with your phone call etiquette and performance, I've included a sample script designed to help you gain information and generate clients and referrals.

Sample Script for Clients and Referrals

"Hello, (Name). This is (Your Name) from (Brokerage). First, I wanted to reach out and see if you're in need of any real estate services or if you're looking to buy or sell any time soon."

If they respond "Yes"—congratulations, you have new business coming in! If they aren't in need of your services, continue.

"I understand. I also wanted to let you know I'm updating my real estate mailing list, and was wondering if you would like to be added / still like to be included?"

If they respond "Yes," continue.

"Great! So you don't consider yourself the client of another agent currently?"

If they respond "No," continue.

"Okay, wonderful—I'd be happy to help when you're ready. Also, would you mind referring me to any friends, relatives, or colleagues who might need an agent? The reason I ask is that I build my real estate business through referrals and I'd love to offer my services to them."

If they respond "Yes," continue.

"Do you have anyone in mind who might be looking for an agent right now?"

If they respond "Yes," continue.

"I'd love to contact them directly to get the conversation started. Would it be possible to pass along their information to me?"

If they respond "Yes," you have a hot lead to a direct referral. If they aren't comfortable passing along the info, say . . .

"I understand. Perhaps I can send you an email with all my information and you can pass it along to them?"

After they have agreed to send you referrals or to continue with you as their agent, make sure to thank them for their business and for their time.

"It was great speaking with you, and thank you so much for your time and for the referral(s). I'm looking forward to working with you again soon!"

As always, follow up! If you haven't heard from your referral, or from the client who agreed to pass along your information in a week, shoot them a quick text or email, or give them a quick phone call.

Sample Script for Cold-Call Client and Referral

"Hi, (Name). This is (Your Name) from (Brokerage). The reason I'm calling is that I wanted to reach out to you and see if you are in need of a real estate agent at the moment."

If they answer "Yes"—great! You have a hot lead. If they answer "No," continue.

"Do you have a real estate agent you currently work with?"

After they answer "Yes" or "No," continue.

"I understand. I'd love to send you a little information about myself and my team. We are completely revolutionizing the real estate industry and we have some exciting news to share with you. Do you have a preferred email address?"

Input their email address into CRM.

"Thanks so much for your time. Before I go, I was wondering if you might have any friends, relatives, or colleagues who are looking for an agent? The reason I ask is that I build my real estate business through referrals and I'd love to offer my services to them."

If they respond "Yes," continue.

"I'd like to contact them directly to get the conversation started. Would it be possible to pass along their information to me?"

If they respond "Yes," you have a hot lead to a direct referral. If they aren't comfortable passing along the info, say . . .

"I understand. Perhaps I can send you an email with all my information and you can pass it along to them?"

"Great! I'm looking forward to working with you, your friends, and your family in the future! Please don't hesitate to contact me with any questions you may have."

Sample Script for Prospective Agents

"Hello, (Name). This is (Your Name) from Agentinc. I wanted to reach out to see if you're interested in changing brokerages."

After they answer "Yes" or "No," continue.

"I see. The reason that I ask is that Agentinc. is a progressive, agent-centric real estate company built by renowned industry expert John McMonigle. Basically, the company is set up to enhance your chances of success through our proprietary technology and cutting-edge marketing campaigns. We also offer several programs to generate passive income between listings, ensuring that you're always bringing in revenue. I'd love to send over some information for you to take a look at, or perhaps we can set up a lunch to discuss?"

If they answer "Yes," continue.

"Great! Also, might you have any colleagues who may be interested in joining us at Agentinc.? It's one of the fastest-growing agencies in the country and we're always looking for like-minded agents.

"Thank you so much for your time. I'm certain you'll enjoy all the perks Agentinc. has to offer. We'll talk soon!"

Human interaction and human connection are the core of our communal happiness. When we achieve connections with clients and are able to serve, we are generating collective joy. One of the simplest ways to expand your connections with your community is to strike up a conversation with someone new who lives in your farm, offer your services, and hand the resident your card.

Each morning when I get dressed, I place 10 business cards in my pocket and I find an opportunity to give away each one of them. At the end of the day, if I still have a card in my pocket, I know I haven't succeeded at connecting with the people I am dedicated to serving.

Remember, this exercise isn't about casually dropping a business card off at a shop or leaving it on a restaurant table after you've finished eating. That practice will get you nowhere. Think of your business cards as a conversation starter. They are a quick and intimate way to engage with potential clients, putting your face to a name and creating a memory. In human interaction, first impressions are solidified within seconds. The best way to ensure that you come across as a professional and make a positive impression is to design a casual "quick pitch" for every card you give away. This pitch shouldn't be a hard sale, nor should it be a flighty remark. Instead, tell people you are a neighborhood specialist and would love to share your knowledge and expertise with them.

Aside from your quick pitch, always have a list of questions to engage people personally, giving you a chance to glean information and learn more about their preferences and needs.

Here are a few things to ask people about that will help you gather the necessary information to create a personal and professional relationship:

1. Ask what neighborhood they live in.
2. Inquire about nearby homes for sale.
3. Ask about any community news.
4. If they have children, ask how their kids are doing in school or in sports.
5. Inquire where they've been dining lately.
6. Ask if you might be able to contact them in a few weeks to see how they're doing.
7. Ask if you can send more information to them.
8. Ask if anyone they know needs an agent.

A successful real estate business is based on personal relationships, and the only way to create a personal relationship is to be personable, caring, and informative.

And remember, once you've successfully distributed your business cards, follow up!

"And remember, once you've successfully distributed your business cards, follow up!"

Financial Health Assessment ✦

0-1 doesn't match   2-3 partial match   4-5 strong match   x put check mark in the related box

I tithe at least 10% weekly.

`0` `1` `2` `3` `4` `5`

I use my money to help others when I can.

`0` `1` `2` `3` `4` `5`

Love Aspects To Focus On ✦
Financial Health

Recommended Reading ✦
God's Power to Change Your Life

Daily Schedule, Day 32.

AM		PM	
06.00	His Word, First Word, Prayer	12.00	
07.00	Exercise	01.00	Scheduled Client/Agent Lunch
08.00	Gather a List of Prospective Contacts	02.00	
09.00		03.00	
10.00	20 Phone Calls	04.00	
11.00		05.00	
		06.00	Home with Family
		07.00	
		08.00	His Word, Last Word, Prayer

THE POWER OF GREAT NEGOTIATING

A new commandment I give to you, that you love one another, even as I have loved you, that you also love one another. (NASB)

John 13:34

He who handles a matter wisely will find good, and whoever trusts in the Lord, happy is he. (MEV)

Proverbs 16:20

Let us never negotiate out of fear. But let us never fear to negotiate.

John F. Kennedy

All of your real estate clients want the same thing: the best possible price. Your sellers will put their faith and trust in you to sell their home at top dollar, and your buyers will put their faith and trust in you to get them their ideal home at the lowest price possible. In order to meet the demands of both types of clients, especially your sellers, you need to understand the power of negotiating.

I'm sure this isn't news to you. Obviously, your ability to negotiate is a powerful differentiator when it comes to building your
career. Many people think or pretend that they are "expert negoti-
ators." It's in their bios, it's on their business cards, it's in their mail
campaigns. But not everyone is. That would be impossible.

But what if I could give you the one thing that would make
you successful? I'm sure you're skeptical that this one thing exists,
because nobody seems to know what this one thing is. Thousands
of books have been written on the subject. Millions of podcasts talk
about it. Agents boast about it on reality television shows. But still,
no one truly understands what it takes to become successful and
become a truly masterful negotiator.

But here's the secret—your ability to become an expert negotiator doesn't come from a promise found in a Tony Robbins book or
a Tom Ferry podcast. It comes from a promise from God.

Take a look at Joshua 1:8:

> This book of the law shall not depart from your mouth, but
> you shall meditate on it day and night, so that you may
> be careful to do according to all that is written in it. For
> then you will make your way prosperous, and you will have
> good success. (ESV)

In Joshua 1:8, God is promising us that if we bind His Scripture to our hearts, we will be successful. It's that simple.

So as we look at the power of great negotiating alongside everything else in our lives and careers, we should also turn to Scripture.

I Corinthians 13:13 is a message from Jesus:

> So now faith, hope, and love abide, these three; but the
> greatest of these is love. (ESV)

Now, let's apply Jesus's message of love, faith, and hope to the
power of great negotiating.

Love: Love Your Client and Love Everyone Involved in the Process

If you Google "negotiations" you'll find thousands of podcasts, clinics, and books on the subject. You'll see and hear words like:

Emotional intelligence
Tactical empathy

Quite frankly, these humanistic views lead to the same place as love, faith, and hope. Start by taking a true interest in the person across the table from you. Look into their eyes. Appreciate their thoughts and emotions. Understand where they are coming from. If you can truly love that person, the process of negotiating just got easier.

The wisest negotiator who ever lived was King Solomon. When he became king, he asked God to give him wisdom. So God made him the wisest, richest, most famous, and most powerful man to ever walk the earth.

As king, he was tasked with judging a difficult case. Two women stood before him claiming to be the mother of a single infant. King Solomon thought for a moment and notoriously said, "Cut the baby in half and give half to each woman." One of the mothers didn't protest the ruling and declared that if she could not have the baby, then neither of them could. But the other woman begged King Solomon for mercy, imploring him to give the baby to the other woman—anything to save the child's life. King Solomon declared her the rightful mother because of her willingness to give up her child in order to save the child's life. King Solomon had the wisdom to know that through love, the problem would be solved.

Faith: Have Faith in Your Discipline and the Process of Negotiating

- **Find out what the rules are.**
  Listening and showing respect are key to engagement.

- **Respect the rules.**
  Showing the other party you are acknowledging and respecting their rules, boundaries, and ultimatums is important to achieve traction and move the ball down the court.
- **Always leave room for margin.**
  Never box yourself into an absolute if it can be avoided. You may have an absolute, but don't give it up too early.
- **Put your best foot forward.**
  To become an expert negotiator and to be successful in your business, you must get people to like you, or at the very least, respect you.
- **Do not sell fear.**
  These are some examples of selling fear:

  > Another offer is coming in.
  > The sky is falling.

  This tactic is too prevalent in our industry and clients are cynical about it. If you try to prey on people's fears, you lose credibility and trust. Even if these scenarios are true and the sky is falling, be careful how you approach your client.

Hope: Have Hope in the Reward

Know that by utilizing Scripture as well as the countercultural messages of love, hope, and faith, you are negotiating with everyone's best interest in mind, which gives you the power to create a successful transaction.

- **Influence the outcome.**
  Take time to imagine all aspects and angles of the upside for each party. Sit in a quiet place and ask yourself this question: How can this scenario benefit who I am negotiating with? Remember, failing to prepare is preparing to fail.

- **Paint a blue sky.**
  If we look to the Old Testament, there is a reference to an "agent." Back then, an agent's duty was to negotiate a wedding. The agent would arrive with gifts of love (treasures) and spend hours and days practicing his disciplines of selling hope in the family who had sent him and generating faith in the bond of marriage. The agent used love, faith, and hope to bring people together for an eternity, in what is most likely the most powerful and important negotiation one can embark upon.

Practical Matters

Now let's discuss practical matters when it comes to negotiating.

We sell in a marketplace where values are subjective. It's like selling Picassos. For instance, who is to say that a property is worth $9M or $12M? When I go after a listing, I always use a range of values and offer three different suggested listing prices with corresponding anticipated shelf life, which of course is a SWAG (silly, wild-ass guess). I also add a replacement breakdown of land and structure to give the valuation a foundation.

I say all this because buyers and sellers in this price range are opinionated, strong-willed, and rash at times. In such instances, it's common to witness narcissistic behavioral patterns on both sides of the transaction. So how do we navigate these waters between two outspoken or stubborn entities? How do we, as agents, drag it all across the finish line?

First, you must have a conviction that buying this home is good for the buyer, whether or not you represent the buyer or seller. A great way to make sure it is a good purchase is to do some research. What was that same house worth 10 years ago? What was it worth 20 years ago? What was it worth 30 years ago? Think about what you are offering—a future investment that will assuredly appreciate over time, possibly by several hundreds of thousands or millions of dollars. If you can find a way to work with the seller to bridge the gap between a few percentage points on the sale, years later you will be praised for making the deal. You will have played a very important role in increasing the wealth of the buyer, while simultaneously meeting the seller's immediate needs or transition goal. But first, you must have the conviction to keep the deal alive. If agents worked together more often, they'd have a larger percentage of successful deals each year.

Second, since we recognize that value is somewhat subjective, getting a deal done is largely psychological. In addition, sellers sometimes ask me what their home is worth, and I will say that it depends on what buyer profile shows up. In other words, being perceptive about putting a deal together is as important as the psychology. Here's an example: In the same coastal luxury building, I did two very different kinds of transactions on similar units last year. The two buyers that showed up could not have been more different, and they differed in two key ways:

Very wealthy buyer versus very conservative buyer stretching
    to pay cash
Buyer who is not in need of a home versus buyer who sold
    their previous home and/or is in emotional need of finding
    a new one

Here are a few points I'd like to make about each experience:

1. **The work begins when you hear the word *no*.**
   Don't ever say the words "Don't shoot the messenger."
   Why? Because messengers don't get paid hundreds of thousands of dollars. I see too many agents quit nudging when their client says no. It's best to always push for a counter. Your value as an agent can be defined by your ability to calmly persuade a client to move toward a qualified buyer or seller in some increment.

2. **Overshoot and undershoot.**
   This goes back to subjective values and the psychology of satisfaction. Here's an example: I was showing a pocket-listing bayfront home to a buyer. The asking price was

$20M. I was aware that the seller's bottom line was $20M. I knew at that moment that the deal would never come together. Therefore, an asking price that provided some margin needed to be placed out there. I have made a habit of always overshooting the threshold to the buyer and undershooting the potential reality for the seller because the satisfaction of getting the "right deal" is the magic at the end of the day.

This brings me to commission. I have two suggestions:

1. Move toward your party in very small increments if needed.
2. Overshoot by not starting with a less-than-standard commission.

But no matter where you find yourself in a negotiation, remember that God has given you the power to create a successful transaction. Utilize the power of love, faith, and hope as you interact with each party in your negotiations.

Financial Health Assessment +

0-1 doesn't match   2-3 partial match   4-5 strong match   x put check mark in the related box

I believe the promises of Scripture, and understand God intends me to be financially responsible and successful.

0 1 2 3 4 5

Love Aspects To Focus On +
Financial Health

Recommended Reading +
God's Power to Change Your Life

Daily Schedule, Day 33.

AM	PM
06.00 His Word, First Word, Prayer	12.00 Networking Lunch
07.00 Exercise	01.00
08.00 Pass out Business Cards	02.00 Pass out Business Cards
09.00	03.00
10.00	04.00
11.00	05.00
	06.00 Home with Family
	07.00
	08.00 His Word, Last Word, Prayer

REVENUE SHARE

And let us consider how we may spur one another on toward love and good deeds, not giving up meeting together, as some are in the habit of doing, but encouraging one another—and all the more as you see the Day approaching. (NIV)

Hebrews 10:24–25

As a faith-based member of the real estate community and as an agent, you need to reach out to those around you who are looking for an opportunity to expand their own careers. As you know, one of the major differentiators of Agentinc. is its revolutionary Revenue Share Program, which allows you to generate passive income between listings, build brand recognition, and solidify your stronghold in your farm and geographic region.

As I mentioned before, being a successful agent isn't just about selling houses—it's about expanding your income opportunities. As an Agentinc. agent, you should focus not only on filling up your CRM with potential clients but also on connecting and networking with potential Agentinc. agents. By dedicating a day to creating a "potential agent CRM" and spending a few hours each week on recruiting new agents, you are effectively building a solid financial future in which you can continuously pad your income.

The Agentinc. Revenue Share Program is designed to generate passive income between escrow closings. As you can see from the following graph, the potential to earn income in ways other than selling homes and representing buyers can be great.

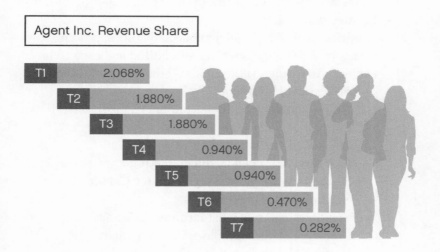

It's easy to see just what Agentinc.'s Revenue Share can do for you when it comes to passive income—but how do you recruit new agents to join Agentinc.?

First, as with everything in real estate, it's important to network. Introduce yourself to other agents—even the competitors in and around your farm—and ask if they'd be interested in learning about what makes Agentinc. one of the fastest-growing and successful agencies in the country. Hand out business cards at open houses and broker previews. Explain that Agentinc. incentivizes growth through providing listing opportunities, enabling agents to become neighborhood specialists, helping agents create revolutionary and proprietary marketing campaigns, and recruiting the finest agents around the world.

Second, put together an email drip campaign for nearby agents that touches upon Agentinc.'s key differentiators:

- **Revenue Share**
  Agentinc.'s Revenue Share Program is designed to award agents residual income based on an actual, transparent percentage, giving agents the ability to actively participate in the financial growth and success of the global Agentinc. brand.
- **Luxury marketing**
  Agentinc.'s effective, multichannel marketing approach allows agents to reach a dynamic yet specialized audience to bring exposure to listings, the agents, and the Agentinc. brand.
  — Professional branding
  — High-impression television and social media advertising
  — Personalized *Elevated* magazine
  — Free social media templates
  — Free targeted social media marketing
  — State-of-the-art marketing Resource Center
  — Neighborhood specialist ads
  — Neighborhood specialist farming assistance
  — Professional photography and videography
  — Professional copywriting
  — Massive exposure through OBEO Unlimited and ListHub
- **Neighborhood geographic farming technology**
  Agentinc.'s neighborhood specialist feature allows agents to claim a neighborhood and connect with vendors and services. By becoming a neighborhood specialist, you can widen your reach, expand your clientele, and generate the trust and confidence necessary to set yourself apart and increase volume.
  — Join the Agentinc. neighborhood specialist program.
  — Use our complex proprietary software that increases agent presence in the geographic farms agents cover.

- Select a geographic farm and maintain a time-proven real estate strategy leveraged by the latest technology.
- Double, or possibly triple, your sales.

- **Sponsored digital marketing**
Agentinc.'s sponsored digital marketing increases visibility and expands brand recognition. Sponsored digital marketing allows agents to showcase listings across a vast yet targeted audience.

- **Resource Center**
Agentinc.'s Resource Center provides agents with everything they need to expand market and farm presence.
  - Agentinc. companies offer the full suite of real estate services.
  - Agents can earn additional revenue by utilizing:
    + Agent Auction
    + Agent Vacation Rental
    + Agent Staging

- **Build your own publication**
Agentinc.'s industry-savvy publication, *Elevated*, keeps your farm up-to-date on the latest real estate trends and activities.
  - Personalized *Elevated* magazine
  - Instant credibility for agent

- **Ground-floor opportunity**
Agentinc. is one of the fastest-growing real estate companies in the country and continues to expand both domestically and globally.
  - Stock options
  - Opportunity to grow exponentially with the company through revenue sharing.

"The key to creating passive income through Agentinc.'s
Revenue Share Program is to find the perfect
balance of recruiting and contacting leads."

The key to creating passive income through Agentinc.'s Revenue Share Program is to find the perfect balance of recruiting and contacting leads. By understanding that you have the power to increase income simply by reaching out to your colleagues and building your own brand, you can strengthen Agentinc.'s presence, create a team atmosphere, and move closer to your financial goals.

Financial Health Assessment ✦
0-1 doesn't match 2-3 partial match 4-5 strong match x put check mark in the related box

I use the talents God gave me to expand my finances and my career opportunities.

☒ 0 ☒ 1 ☒ 2 ☒ 3 ☐ 4 ☒ 5

I consistently set financial goals for myself and meet them.

☒ 0 ☒ 1 ☒ 2 ☒ 3 ☒ 4 ☒ 5

Love Aspects To Focus On ✦
Financial Health

Recommended Reading ✦
Financial Fitness

Daily Schedule, Day 34.

AM	
06.00	His Word, First Word, Prayer
07.00	Exercise
08.00	
09.00	Reach Out to At Least 3 Agents About Revenue Share Program
10.00	
11.00	

PM	
12.00	Networking Lunch
01.00	Agent Inc. Social Media Posts
02.00	
03.00	
04.00	
05.00	
06.00	Home with Family
07.00	
08.00	His Word, Last Word, Prayer

BE A SHOWMAN OR
SHOW WOMAN

Or do you not know that your body is a temple of the Holy Spirit within you, whom you have from God? You are not your own, for you were bought with a price. So glorify God in your body. (ESV)

1 Corinthians 6:19–20

God created us in His image and intends us to bring love, hope, and faith to others. He also expects us to respect and cherish our bodies, to be the best we can be both physically and mentally, and to use our talents to the best of our abilities.

There is a saying—"Success follows success." As humans, we see with our eyes first, and often we make quick judgments based upon what we see. Our judgments may not always be correct, but a good first impression can go a long way toward gaining clients and cultivating client trust.

When it comes to your appearance, I find that one of the easiest ways to attract clients and convey professionalism is maintaining an up-to-date wardrobe and grooming regimen.

When I started out as an agent, I always made sure I wore a tailored suit and drove a car that suited my own personal financial and professional expectations. While I may have lived beyond my means momentarily, my dedication to showmanship created an aura of success that followed me, allowing me to create a reputation fitting my dedication to selling real estate and taking care of clients. Remember, as an agent you are tasked with helping people make one of the biggest investments of their lives. In order for you to gain their trust, they must believe that you are successful at what you do. They must feel confident that you have the ability to guide them and that you have successfully guided other clients as well.

Whether or not you know it, as an agent, you are onstage. People are watching you at open houses, at restaurants, at broker previews—even at the grocery store. Agents are leaders in their communities, and as a leader, you have the responsibility to present yourself with respect and pride. In this business, your ability to differentiate yourself as a confident and successful leader can mean the difference between winning a client and losing one. That's why everything you can do to put forth the best representation of yourself, even physically, is of the utmost importance. Remember, when you take good care of yourself, you are telling your clients you can take good care of them as well.

Here are a few pointers on becoming a showman or show woman:

- **Always be well groomed.**
  Get a haircut. Shave. Pluck your eyebrows. Whiten your teeth. Trim your nails. All of these seemingly minor details can have a major effect when it comes to a client's first impression—and all of these grooming practices are easy to maintain.
- **Select a current and professional wardrobe.**
  By looking your best and wearing clothing that demands attention and respect, you are presenting yourself as someone who is both dedicated to their career and successful at it.

"By looking your best and wearing clothing that demands attention and respect, you are presenting yourself as someone who is both dedicated to their career and successful at it."

- **Buy yourself a nice car or properly maintain your car.**
  Your car will be parked in your farm every single day you are working. The people in your farm will look at your car and they will judge you: Is this agent successful? Is this agent serious about handling my investments? Is this agent capable of generating the future and wealth I desire for myself and my family? I don't believe it is wise to purchase items that may have a negative impact on your financial situation. Living within your means is crucial to maintaining a successful business. However, if you find yourself able to afford a car that you will enjoy and that will empower you, go ahead and treat yourself. If you aren't in that position, don't worry about it. Just make sure your car is always clean and well maintained—the way you treat your possessions speaks volumes about how you will treat your clients.
- **Exercise and eat healthy.**
  We can't all look like Brad Pitt—that's a fact. But regular exercise can not only help improve physical appearance and increase confidence, but also lower stress, create energy, elevate your mood, and generate positivity both outwardly and inwardly. God gave us these bodies to do good work with—it's up to us to ensure that our bodies are able to carry out the promises we have made to Him in our partnership, as well as the promises we have made to ourselves and our families.

Financial Health Assessment ✦

0-1 doesn't match   2-3 partial match   4-5 strong match   x put check mark in the related box

I avoid unnecessary debt whenever I can.

`[0]` `[1]` `[2]` `[3]` `[4]` `[5]`

I am open to all opportunities when it comes to my financial wellbeing, and make my financial decisions based on the teachings of Christ.

`[0]` `[1]` `[2]` `[3]` `[4]` `[5]`

Love Aspects To Focus On ✦   Recommended Reading ✦
Financial Health   Financial Fitness

Daily Schedule, Day 35. 🕐

AM		PM	
06.00	His Word, First Word, Prayer	12.00	Networking Lunch
07.00	Exercise	01.00	Wardrobe Shopping
08.00	Grooming Appointment	02.00	
09.00	Research New Car/ Car Maintenance	03.00	
10.00		04.00	
11.00		05.00	
		06.00	Home with Family
		07.00	
		08.00	His Word, Last Word, Prayer

CREATE MARGIN IN YOUR SCHEDULE

Teach us to number our days, that we may gain a heart of wisdom. (NIV)

Psalm 90:12

In our industry, it's both extremely easy and extremely common to lose ourselves in our work. As an agent, we do not work 8 hours a day. We don't punch in at 9 and punch out at 5. Some of us work 7 days a week, 18 hours a day—but what will that get you, and at what cost? God didn't create you to become a real estate robot. In fact, He expects us to take time to relax, to enjoy the world He has created, to experience love, to spend time with family, to witness the joy of others, and to spend time with Him and the Christian community.

In order to understand the importance of rest and creating a margin in your schedule, let's take a look at Scripture and the Ten Commandments. Commandment number four tells us, "Remember the Sabbath day, to keep it holy. Six days you shall labor, and do all your work, but the seventh day is a Sabbath to the Lord your God." (ESV)

Isaiah 58:13–14 reads:

> If you turn back your foot from the Sabbath, from doing your pleasure on my holy day, and call the Sabbath a delight and the holy day of the Lord honorable; if you honor it, not going your own ways, or seeking our own pleasure, or talking idly; then you shall take delight in the Lord, and I will make you ride on the heights of the earth; I will feed you with the heritage of Jacob your father, for the mouth of the Lord has spoken. (ESV)

These are pretty straightforward messages and promises. God created the Sabbath to ensure that we find time to enjoy His presence and the world He created. He created the Sabbath so that we could take one full day of the week to put Him first and to delight in the joy and beauty that He has surrounded us with.

In 2009, I had over $800M in listings. I was making an eight-figure income. I lived in a $10.25M house. I had just completed a $14M freestanding Class A limestone office building for my brokerage located in the heart of Newport Beach at 1000 Newport Center Drive. I drove exotic cars; had an inordinately large watch collection; owned second, third, and fourth homes; traveled by private jet everywhere; and had built a net worth of $70M. I was convinced that my nonstop work ethic and lavish lifestyle were essential for my family's security and future. In fact, the trajectory my life had taken—from arriving on Lido Isle with $73 in my pocket to making eight figures—made me want to write what would have been the first version of this book. That version would have been titled *All the Right Moves*, and it would have brashly and confidently showcased all my secrets to becoming a real estate juggernaut.

"I immersed myself in prayer and I began to exercise. I made
a decision to give my heart back to God, to acknowledge
that He is the rightful owner of my body and my life."

But within a few days of coming up with my book idea, my world of opulence and success came crashing down with an epic thud. The market crashed. My construction lender was seized by the FDIC. Millions of dollars vanished overnight. My wife left me. And within weeks, I was facing bankruptcy. I was living a prideful life based on the accumulation of material wealth and driven by ego—not a life based on servitude—and due to my pride, blind ambition, and materialism, God removed His protective hedge from my life.

I had stopped putting God first. I wasn't faithfully observing the Sabbath. Sure, I would attend church, but then I'd hold open houses, write contracts, and attend showings. Not only that, but I wasn't tithing 10 percent or praying to God about big decisions. If I wanted something, I simply chased it and acquired it in defiance of God's divine will for my life. My heart wasn't operating as God had envisioned. I had stolen my heart from God and turned it against Him. I wasn't following my heart, listening to my heart, or allowing God's presence within my heart. In short, my heart was failing. But, lucky for me and for us all, God is in the heart transplant business. During this period of extreme hardship, inner turmoil, and financial ruin, I turned to the Bible. I immersed myself in prayer and I began to exercise. I decided to give my heart back to God, to acknowledge that He is the rightful owner of my body and my life. With each new day, my heart strengthened. With each new day, my heart expanded. With each new day, my heart became one again with God. God began new work in my body, my soul, and my life. And now, I see it all growing each day.

Today, I understand that my experience of loss and hardship was a blessing. At the peak of my financial success, I had all but ignored the most important part of being alive—being true to myself and to my family. When we aspire to greatness, wealth, and power, we can lose sight of what it means to take a deep breath and look around. We can lose sight of what we appreciate most because we are convinced that these "things" will bring happiness not only to ourselves but also to those around us. The truth is, God wants us to make money—but He also wants us to embody loving-kindness. He wants us to lead by example. He wants us to lead with service. And he wants us to always put Him first and regularly pay Him His share of the profits!

As I began to pick up the pieces and put my career and life back together, I made a conscious and deliberate decision to never again let my life be controlled by my career, my pride, or my ego. I decided to spend more time on what matters most in life—my family, my loved ones, my friends, and my faith. Now, Agentinc. is one of the fastest-growing real estate companies in the nation—and I built it by taking the necessary time each day to do what matters most.

This book exists to give agents an opportunity to find the perfect work-life balance. It is a guide to becoming your best self, both financially and personally. By taking time out of your schedule to pray, exercise, read the Bible, and inject joy into the lives of those around you, you are creating a lifestyle that is rich in love—and love is the most priceless possession on earth.

When we create time to visit with the people we love and to do the things we love that are completely separate from our career aspirations and financial expectations, we are in tune with what God envisioned for our existence. A life lived lost in ego and obsessed with possessing and accumulating wealth is a life void of love.

I know what many of you are thinking: "I have no time to do it all. How can I pray, spend time with my family, attend ballet recitals, do the grocery shopping, be a loving husband, be a loving wife?" But you have the time, and you can do and be all those things and more.

Here are a few ways you can create margin in your schedule while still working toward your career goals:

1. **Take some time between meetings.**
    Fight the temptation to fill your day with meetings, show-ings, and phone calls. Make sure you have at least 15 to 30 minutes to switch gears, refocus, rest, eat, or exercise. When you feel relaxed, positive, and rested, the world notices and you attract success.

2. **Take a healthy lunch break.**
    It sounds simple—stop and eat. But many of us are on the run each day. We opt for unhealthy options—drive-through or takeout. Or we simply don't eat. Our bodies are sacred. One of the easiest ways to respect yourself is by taking the time to eat a healthy meal and clear your mind. A quick lit-tle break in the middle of the day will give you the energy and confidence you need to complete your tasks.

3. **Spend time with a loved one or friend.**
    You don't need to schedule a long lunch with everyone in your life each day. A quick phone call to check in on your husband, wife, sons, daughters, or other family members can lift your spirits, keep you grounded, and reaffirm why it is you have chosen this profession.

4. **Define your end time.**
    We all have the tendency to want to answer emails, texts, and phone calls at all hours of the day. While it is import-ant to be available to your clients, it is also important to set boundaries. You need time for yourself. And your family needs time with you. Set a time of day to pull yourself away from the computer or phone and spend time with those you love, doing what you love. Life is a two-way street: you can have it all, and then it can be taken away. But your life and your loved ones will always be there—and that is where your true riches lie.

Vocational Health Assessment ✦

0-1 doesn't match   2-3 partial match   4-5 strong match   x put check mark in the related box

I praise God during difficult times and learn from my adversity.

`0` `1` `2` `3` `4` `5`

My decisions as an agent are modeled after the teachings of Christ.

`0` `1` `2` `3` `4` `5`

I regularly use my time to serve God.

`0` `1` `2` `3` `4` `5`

Love Aspects To Focus On ✦   Recommended Reading ✦
Vocational Health   Financial Fitness

Daily Schedule, Day 36.

AM		PM	
06.00	His Word, First Word, Prayer	12.00	Networking Lunch
07.00	Exercise	01.00	Interaction with Loved One
08.00	Work on Schedule and Create Your Margins	02.00	
09.00		03.00	
10.00		04.00	
11.00		05.00	
		06.00	Home with Family
		07.00	
		08.00	His Word, Last Word, Prayer

FINANCIAL FITNESS

"Bring the whole tithe into the storehouse, that there may be food in my house. Test me in this," says the Lord Almighty, "and see if I will not throw open the floodgates of heaven and pour out so much blessing that there will not be room enough to store it." (NIV)

Malachi 3:10

The Bible is filled with financial advice. In fact, there are more Bible passages focused on money and finances than on any other subject. Now, you may be asking yourself why the Bible is so chock-full of financial guidance to begin with. "Isn't the message of God and Jesus to love one another, work toward peace, and live a life of stewardship?" Yes, it is. But God also understands that the world, universe, and kingdom He created involve investing in your eternal future—not only monetarily but with your actions, your spirit, your love, your kindness, and your willingness to dedicate yourself to your faith.

It is with these "spiritual investments" that you create wealth in God's kingdom. And when you generate wealth in God's kingdom, God will yield eternal dividends.

Earlier on in your journey, you consecrated your business. You gave your business to God and made Him a partner in your financial future. This vow is binding in His kingdom, just as a partnership in California or Ohio or Kentucky or Barcelona is here on earth. When we make a business agreement with a partner, we are expected to uphold our end of the deal, or there will be consequences.

If you wish for God to bless your finances, then you must put Him above all else when it comes to money. I grew up Baptist in a family with very little money—but we were rich in faith. Though my father struggled to make ends meet, he taught me the principles of tithing and saving. He was responsible financially and he was generous with his tithing. Each time money came in, 10 percent went to the church and 10 percent went into savings. This 10 and 10 principle became ingrained in me at a young age—though over the years, I lost sight of its importance. I went to college, began working, started out in real estate, and before I knew it, this simple yet incredibly important aspect of my financial faith disappeared.

Pastor Rick Warren, in his workshop titled "Financial Fitness," lays out fundamental ways for us to increase our equity both here on earth and in the Kingdom of Heaven. His teachings and insights on why it is important to place your financial trust in God before all else have allowed me to rebuild my own financial future and successfully attain my goals.

"This is why budgeting, saving, and tithing is
so important to a financially fit future."

He speaks of seven foundations of financial freedom:*

Possession
Allocation
Accountability
Utilization
Motivation
Application
Compensation

I want you to do something right now—reach in your wallet and pull out a $1 bill and flip it on its back. What do you see? A pyramid on one side representing strength and duration, and wings on the other side representing the will of your dollar to fly away from your pocket! This is why budgeting, saving, and tithing are so important to a financially fit future. If you let your money take flight and land someplace both you and your Divine Partner don't want it to land, then you are mismanaging your finances and placing yourself in a direct business conflict with God. And we all know who will win that battle not only here on earth but also in the Kingdom of Heaven.

When it came time to create Agentinc., I knew I had to forge a powerful partnership with God and the church to establish a budget and business plan that would last me not only through my life here on earth but also throughout eternity. I promised God that my new company would not be focused solely on myself and my own worth—it would be dedicated to investing in my eternal future as well as creating a path for those around me to succeed today, tomorrow, and eternally.

During my first months launching Agentinc., there were times when I would look at my bank account in horror, wondering where

---

* Visit https://pastorrick.com/series/financial-fitness/ to learn more about Pastor Rick's faith-based financial guidance.

all the money was going and when it would finally come back in. But I made a promise to God when I consecrated my business—I would give Him 10 percent of everything I had in return for His partnership. Now, most people would have abandoned this practice during such a tumultuous financial time—and in my younger days, I may have done just that. But today, I realize what we are planning for here on earth is only one very small blip in our eternal journey. When we come to learn that our partnership with God is stronger than a partnership with Elon Musk or Mark Cuban, we can act progressively in our financial decisions. That's why Agentinc. has created an ever-evolving and consistently updated digital budget tool for all agents to remain on track when it comes to managing your business and finances. Visit www.agentbudget.co to get started!

The day you consecrated your business, you read the Parable of the Talents. In it, we discover that God expects us to invest the money we make in our futures both here on earth and in the Kingdom of Heaven:

> For whoever has, will be given more, and they will have an abundance. Whoever does not have, even what they have, will be taken from them. And throw that worthless servant outside, into the darkness, where there will be weeping and gnashing of teeth. (NIV)

Money is not to be stockpiled. It is to be spent to better ourselves and those around us. After listening to Pastor Rick Warren, I began to understand that the last person I wanted to owe money to was God. God is actually looking for people to bless. In Scripture, He made over 7,000 promises, including ones that tell us how to use our money wisely. By tithing 10 percent and saving 10 percent, no matter what your monthly income may be, you are showing God, your community, and your family where your heart truly is. Remember, if you want God to transform your heart, your eternal future, and your finances, then you must give back to Him.

As I've explained before, real estate is a two-way street. Your service to clients yields rewards in your business just as your faith, tithing, and commitment to God's partnership will yield rewards in heaven.

It's important to always remember that everything you have belongs to God. By devoting yourself financially to God, to the betterment of others, and to the world as a whole, you are epitomizing Christian stewardship and staying true to the business commitments and promises you have made to your most important partner.

Vocational Health Assessment ✦

0-1 doesn't match   2-3 partial match   4-5 strong match   x put check mark in the related box

I serve God by using the talents he has given me to expand our business.

0️⃣ 1️⃣ 2️⃣ 3️⃣ 4️⃣ 5️⃣

I am open to opportunities that will benefit my community and those around me.

0️⃣ 1️⃣ 2️⃣ 3️⃣ 4️⃣ 5️⃣

I use my career to bring kindness and happiness not only to my clients, but also to everyone I meet.

0️⃣ 1️⃣ 2️⃣ 3️⃣ 4️⃣ 5️⃣

Love Aspects To Focus On ✦
Vocational Health

Recommended Reading ✦
Financial Fitness

Daily Schedule, Day 37. 🕐

AM	PM
06.00 His Word, First Word, Prayer	12.00 Networking Lunch
07.00 Exercise	01.00 Continue Financial Fitness
08.00 Begin Pastor Rick Warren's Financial Fitness	02.00
09.00	03.00
10.00	04.00
11.00	05.00
	06.00 Home with Family
	07.00
	08.00 His Word, Last Word, Prayer

SET YOURSELF APART AS A NEIGHBORHOOD SPECIALIST WITH A GRAPHIC MAP OF YOUR FARM

Your word is a lamp to my feet and a light to my path. (ESV)
Psalm 119:105

G od has given us a map to follow in our lives—Scripture. His words are a lamp to our feet and a light to our path. In life, we all need a map to find our way, whether it's to a new restaurant or a new career. Throughout eternity, maps have led us to discover new worlds, new sciences, new thoughts, new loves, and new beginnings. They are an integral piece of our societal framework and an important aspect of our spiritual health. So why not use one to assist you in your real estate career?

In the intensely competitive market of Newport Beach, you can swing a tea towel and hit another agent. In a market like that, it's easy to question your ability to stand out and differentiate yourself from the other agents—how are you going to push your way into the top 5 percent of the agents in your farm?

As I've pointed out repeatedly, it is important to find a distinct way to separate yourself from other agents and establish yourself as the go-to resource and agent in your farm.

When I started out, I focused entirely on becoming the best agent on Lido Isle in Newport Beach, one of the most valuable, highest-profit, and highest-stakes regions in the entire country. But how was I going to gain the trust of my clients? How could I assure them that their multimillion-dollar properties were in the best hands possible? And then it hit me—I could distinguish myself as a neighborhood expert.

By now, you've hopefully claimed a neighborhood with Agentinc. or your brokerage of choice and begun building your vendor list, posting, and connecting with the residents in your farm. Each of these actions is vital to your success in building your clientele. But sometimes we need something extra to help us rise above. That's why I highly recommend creating a graphic map of your farm and keeping it up-to-date with any new listings, amenities, developments, and businesses entering your neighborhood.

If there's a new restaurant opening up in town, point it out on the map. If there are new docks opening up for rental, put a star next to them. Highlight the beaches, the clubhouses, the tennis courts, the parks, the schools—anything of interest to your clients. And place this map on the back of your mailers or brochures, or in the body of emails going out to your CRM. Just as it is invaluable for us as agents to visualize our future, it is important for your buyers to visualize where they want to live and where your sellers' houses are situated. Your buyers may look at the map and say, "I'd like to live near the school." This allows you to save time and focus on searching within a particular area of your farm. Your sellers may look at the map, see the comps, and explore the recent sales in their neighborhood, and say, "The value of my home is greater/less than I expected," which will save you valuable time when it comes to negotiating the asking price and managing expectations.

"Place this map on the back of your mailers or brochures,
or in the body of emails going out to your CRM."

Creating a geographic map not only allows your clients to easily see what is happening in their market but also demonstrates once again your dedication to your craft. When clients see that you are willing to go the extra mile in every aspect of your profession, including building a visual reference that will help them understand each and every amenity of their community, you continue to add value to your brand and business and set yourself apart.

In this highly competitive industry, it is vital to do everything you can to showcase your service and expertise. Again, when your clients feel you have differentiated yourself as an agent who understands not only the value of their assets but also the inner workings of the community they wish to buy or sell in, you have successfully differentiated yourself from your competitors. Sometimes it takes one small extra step to gain a client. Don't you want to take that step?

In order to help you create a successful geographic map, I've highlighted a few amenities to focus on:

Beaches, lakes, rivers, and creeks
Parks, playgrounds, and trails
Fine dining, entertainment, and retail
Schools
Airports
Harbors, marinas, and available dockage
Recent listings and home sales
Gyms
Malls and shopping centers
Specialty grocers

Creating a geographic map can be simple. Take a screenshot of your area, highlight the amenities, and send it to a graphic designer.

Or hire someone to illustrate your map. Continue to add to it throughout the years and use it to help clients understand the area.

Vocational Health Assessment +

0-1 doesn't match   2-3 partial match   4-5 strong match   × put check mark in the related box

I use my platform as an agent to spread the message of God and my faith.

`0` `1` `2` `3` `4` `5`

With each transaction, I do my best to ensure my clients benefit as much as I do.

`0` `1` `2` `3` `4` `5`

My actions are governed by the Word of God.

`0` `1` `2` `3` `4` `5`

Love Aspects To Focus On +   Recommended Reading +
Vocational Health   Financial Fitness

Daily Schedule, Day 38. 🕐

AM		PM	
06.00	His Word, First Word, Prayer	12.00	Networking Lunch
07.00	Exercise	01.00	
08.00	Begin Mapping Your Farm	02.00	Reach Out to Agent Inc. Media Department or Contact a Graphic Designer
09.00		03.00	
10.00		04.00	
11.00		05.00	
		06.00	Home with Family
		07.00	
		08.00	His Word, Last Word, Prayer

BUILD RELATIONSHIPS WITH OTHER AGENTS

But I say to you, love your enemies, bless those who curse you, do good to those who hate you, and pray for those who spitefully use you and persecute you. (MEV)

Matthew 5:44

As agents, we are inherently competitive. Our industry, our markets, and our livelihoods are dependent upon competition to drive sales, gain listings, and generate income. But just because we work in a competitive industry doesn't mean that you should treat other agents as "competition," or even worse, as "enemies." While you are in the field networking, looking for listings, assisting buyers, and building your brand, it is important to know that hostile actions toward other agents never pay off. Over the years, I've seen it all—intense rivalries, bad-mouthing, vicious rumors, sign stealing, misleading clients—all for personal gain. The truth is, if you are able to take the high road, to refrain from the feelings, emotions, and actions that are synonymous with "competition" and "battle," you will become a more successful agent in the long run.

Our industry is based upon reputation—not just with clients but with agents and agencies. Throughout your career, you will encounter other agents who speak down to you or make disparaging comments about you to clients. It is important to be thick-skinned and let these hostilities roll off your back. Love your enemies. Pray for them. Do not engage in "war." Do not satisfy your enemies' hate by returning it with hate. Always take the high road. When you lead by your Christian actions and behavior, you instill a positive image not only in your clients but also in those who work around you and with you.

When dealing with competitors, it's not just about turning down the volume on any negative interactions—it's about forging relationships with them, building an avenue of trust, and exemplifying your dedication to your craft and faith. Today, very few agents work on developing and building lasting relationships with other agents. Some of you may have had a bad experience or relationship early on and have consequently put up walls, closing yourself off to the negative energy that surrounds certain colleagues. Because of these experiences, many of you will neglect creating trustful and possibly financially lucrative relationships with your "enemies." But real estate isn't just about networking your farm—it's about networking your industry. By approaching your "enemies" and "competitors" with love, hope, and faith, you are opening yourself up to greater financial possibilities.

I can guarantee this—as you continue to build relationships with your fellow agents and excel in your farm, you will gain the respect and admiration of your peers, colleagues, and "competitors." As your success and reputation grows, you may find that other agents reach out to you for help, looking at you as an asset rather than an impediment. They may bring a buyer to you or ask you to co-list a property with them to expand their geographic reach and enhance their chance of selling. In order to gain the respect and trust of your fellow agents, you must consistently demonstrate your dedication to professionalism and God.

Conversely, some of you may be starting out and may not have built a firm reputation in your farm yet. So how do you begin building your reputation? Not surprisingly, one of the best ways to gain traction in your farm is to reach out to other agents. Ask if they need help with a listing. Ask if you can hold an open house for them. Ask how you can be of service to them. Ask if there is anything you can do to help them succeed. By investing in your reputation and always acting with respect and class toward fellow agents, you are furthering your brand image and your core business messaging and placing yourself in a positive light that is impossible to ignore. If you can lend a helping hand and generate a commission not just for yourself but also for those who work alongside you, your goodwill will pay off tenfold in the future.

In this industry, there are no "enemies," there is no "competition." Focus on your personal responsibilities and place your faith in your partnership with God.

Here are a few tips to help you remain focused on being a positive and professional agent in your farm:

1. **Don't take it personally.**
   You may find yourself the subject of slanderous comments—pay no attention to them. Remain focused on generating a positive image, rather than dwelling on the negative actions of others. Your dedication to building your reputation as a professional and trustworthy agent is far more important than focusing on what has been said about you.

2. **Practice gratitude.**
   Be thankful that God has given you your brains, your body, and your talents. Thank God each day that He has partnered with you to grow and expand your business. Take a look at the tiniest fragments of your life that make it beautiful.

"Make your journey one of beauty and love, and let others decide how they'd like to embellish their own journey."

---

3. **Understand that everyone has their own journey and life to live.**
   The path you are on is unique. Make your journey one of beauty and love, and let others decide how they'd like to embellish their own journey.

4. **Take some alone time.**
   Sit with yourself and God and understand that you are the loving embodiment of Christ. You are in a very competitive and fast-paced industry, but your willingness to always lead by example will differentiate you and continue to move your career forward.

Vocational Health Assessment ✦
0-1 doesn't match   2-3 partial match   4-5 strong match   x put check mark in the related box

I approach each day and business transaction with love, faith, and hope.

`0` `1` `2` `3` `4` `5`

I love, care for, and encourage those who are less fortunate.

`0` `1` `2` `3` `4` `5`

I am able to forgive and continue forward with grace not only in my personal life, but also in my professional life.

`0` `1` `2` `3` `4` `5`

Love Aspects To Focus On ✦   Recommended Reading ✦
Vocational Health   Financial Fitness

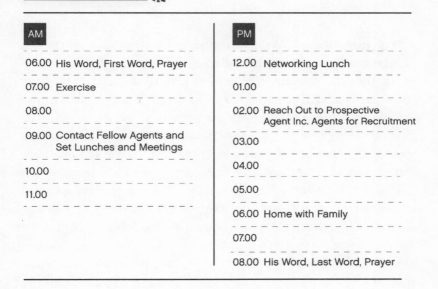

Daily Schedule, Day 39.

AM

06.00 His Word, First Word, Prayer

07.00 Exercise

08.00

09.00 Contact Fellow Agents and Set Lunches and Meetings

10.00

11.00

PM

12.00 Networking Lunch

01.00

02.00 Reach Out to Prospective Agent Inc. Agents for Recruitment

03.00

04.00

05.00

06.00 Home with Family

07.00

08.00 His Word, Last Word, Prayer

PREPARE FOR THE HARVEST

Finish your outdoor work and get your fields ready; after that, build your house. (TLV)

Proverbs 24:27

Congratulations! You have completed your 40-day journey to becoming a successful, positive, spiritual, and professional agent. By taking on the challenge of this 40-day book, you have positioned yourself to become a recipient of the over 7,000 promises of Scripture. You have chosen a life of integrity, of credibility, and of spirituality. You have chosen the path of becoming an upstanding member of your community and a valued neighbor and colleague who acts with stewardship and kindness at the forefront of your intentions. You have consecrated your business and added the most powerful partner in the world as you continue accomplishing your goals and realizing your visions. By taking these essential steps and continuing to remain focused on the lessons and advice provided in this book, you are actively investing not only in your future here on earth but also in your future in God's kingdom.

Now, you may find it difficult to remain on track and disciplined when it comes to the continuous evolution and progress of your career. And when you find yourself falling behind or feeling discouraged, don't worry—everything you need to continue your journey can be found in Scripture. If you read the Bible and pray each morning and each night, you will find all the answers you need to maintain positivity and self-value, while continuing to grow spiritually, personally, and professionally.

All Scripture is God-breathed and is useful for teaching, rebuking, correcting and training in righteousness. (NIV)
2 Timothy 3:16

Remember, God is your partner! Take pride in the strength of your partnership! Respect what He gives you each day! In exchange for His guidance and support, He simply asks you to invest in your eternal future. He wants you to take the wealth He has given you and support your faith through tithing. He wants you to take the wealth He has given you and make it grow. If we look to Scripture, it is clear that God does not oppose wealth— He opposes greed. If we look to Scripture, it is clear that money is to be used as a tool to benefit you and others. Proverbs 10:22 states, "When the Lord blesses you with riches, you have nothing to regret." (CEV) Now is the time to accept God's blessing, to accept His 7,000 promises, and to accept both financial and spiritual health.

We are here on earth as agents to fulfill God's divine will, to support with integrity ourselves and our families, and to provide service to our clients that reflects our Christian beliefs. By assisting our neighbors through the most important financial decisions of their lives, we are exemplifying our dedication to living a life of servitude that will generate eternal rewards and bring love, hope, and faith to ourselves and to our world.

As a fellow agent and follower of Christ, I'd like you to know my ultimate goal is to spend eternity with you in heaven. If you have accepted Christ as your business partner, as your companion, and most of all, as your savior, I'd like to hear the good news! Please feel free to reach out to me anytime. I am devoted to your success both financially and spiritually, and I know that together we can do God's work here on earth so that we may not only enjoy our lives today but also rejoice in the Kingdom of Heaven tomorrow.

> God bless!
> So now you can rejoice. Your past is forgiven,
> You have a purpose for living,
> And you have a house made for you in heaven.

Vocational Health Assessment ✳

0-1 doesn't match   2-3 partial match   4-5 strong match   ✕ put check mark in the related box

I trust God to assist me in my career and in my personal endeavors.

| 0 | 1 | 2 | 3 | 4 | 5 |

I believe I have the ability to transform the lives of those around me.

| 0 | 1 | 2 | 3 | 4 | 5 |

Love Aspects To Focus On ✳   Recommended Reading ✳
Vocational Health   Financial Fitness

Daily Schedule, Day 40. 🕐

AM	
06.00	His Word, First Word, Prayer
07.00	Exercise
08.00	Research Purchasing a Home in Your Farm
09.00	
10.00	
11.00	

PM	
12.00	Networking Lunch
01.00	
02.00	
03.00	
04.00	
05.00	
06.00	Celebrate the Dawn of Your New Career with Family
07.00	
08.00	His Word, Last Word, Prayer

ACKNOWLEDGMENTS

I 'd like to thank my incredibly supportive wife, Hannah, who has helped me realize my vision of building a truly exceptional real estate company built *by* agents *for* agents. Your inspiration and love for our family is truly infinite.

I'd also like to thank my team at Agentinc. who worked with me to bring *40 Days of Farming* to life, including Justin J. Murphy, Lauren Phillips, Caitie Layman, and Joao Baptista.

Thank you to the entire team at BenBella for their insight and expertise—Matt Holt, Katie Dickman, Brigid Pearson, Jay Kilburn, Jennifer Brett Greenstein, and Mallory Hyde.

And finally, thank you to Newport Beach, Corona del Mar, and Sun Valley for providing the perfect home and community for my family and myself for so many years.

ABOUT THE AUTHOR

When it comes to real estate, John McMonigle has seen and done it all. Utilizing a combination of experience, networking, and faith, John has been able to transform the art of geographic real estate farming into a lucrative and time-tested system designed to generate financial and personal success.

Renowned across the nation and throughout the world for his unparalleled expertise, John has made history by selling properties totaling more than $7.5 billion, and has been named the #1 Real Estate Team in the world in multiple years by the *Wall Street Journal*. As the foremost expert in residential real estate and founder of Agentinc., John has been featured in some of the nation's most respected publications, and has appeared on *The Oprah Winfrey Show*, *Access Hollywood*, *The Insider*, HGTV, and most recently was the star of Bravo's *Real Estate Wars*.

John believes everyone can enjoy the same success he has achieved if they are willing to take the necessary steps to grow mentally, physically, and vocationally. In *40 Days of Farming*, John gives his readers all the tools they need to live a fulfilling life both professionally and spiritually.